Grade **1**

Pearson Scott Foresman

Leveled Reader
Teaching Guide

D1401108

Glenview, Illinois • Boston, Massachusetts • Chandler, Arizona • Upper Saddle River, New Jersey

ISBN: 13: 978-0-328-48440-9
ISBN: 10:   0-328-48440-7

2 3 4 5 6 7 8 9 10 V031 13 12 11 10

Table of Contents

LEVELED READER TITLE	Instruction	Comprehension Practice	Vocabulary Practice
Mack and Zack	12–13	14	15
The Sick Pets	16–17	18	19
Where They Live	20–21	22	23
Which Fox?	24–25	26	27
What Animals Can You See?	28–29	30	31
Which Animals Will We See?	32–33	34	35
Let's Go to the Zoo	36–37	38	39
A Class	40–41	42	43
Look at My Neighborhood	44–45	46	47
The Dinosaur Herds	48–49	50	51
People Help the Forest	52–53	54	55
Honey	56–57	58	59
Let's Build a Park	60–61	62	63
Mac Can Do It!	64–65	66	67
Big Wishes and Her Baby	68–69	70	71
Plans Change	72–73	74	75
Let's Visit a Butterfly Greenhouse	76–77	78	79
Seasons Come and Go	80–81	82	83

Graphic Organizers

Introduction

Scott Foresman *Reading Street* provides more than 750 leveled readers that help children become better readers and build a lifelong love of reading. The *Reading Street* leveled readers are engaging texts that help children practice critical reading skills and strategies. They also provide opportunities to build vocabulary, understand concepts, and develop reading fluency.

The leveled readers were developed to be age-appropriate and appealing to children at each grade level. The leveled readers consist of engaging texts in a variety of genres, including fantasy, folk tales, realistic fiction, historical fiction, and narrative and expository nonfiction. To better address real-life reading skills that children will encounter in testing situations and beyond, a higher percentage of nonfiction texts is provided at each grade.

USING THE LEVELED READERS

You can use the leveled readers to meet the diverse needs of your children. Consider using the readers to

- practice critical skills and strategies
- build fluency
- build vocabulary and concepts
- build background for the main selections in the student book
- provide a variety of reading experiences, e.g., shared, group, individual, take-home, readers' theater

GUIDED READING APPROACH

The *Reading Street* leveled readers are leveled according to Guided Reading criteria by experts trained in Guided Reading. The Guided Reading levels increase in difficulty within a grade level and across grade levels. In addition to leveling according to Guided Reading criteria, the instruction provided in the *Leveled Reader Teaching Guide* is compatible with Guided Reading instruction. An instructional routine is provided for each leveled reader. This routine is most effective when working with individual children or small groups.

MANAGING THE CLASSROOM

When using the leveled readers with individuals or small groups, you'll want to keep the other children engaged in meaningful, independent learning tasks. Establishing independent practice stations throughout the classroom and child routines for these stations can help you manage the rest of the class while you work with individuals or small groups. Practice stations can include listening, phonics, vocabulary, independent reading, and cross-curricular activities. For classroom management, create a work board that lists the stations and which children should be at each station. Provide instructions at each station that detail the tasks to be accomplished. Update the board and alert children when they should rotate to a new station. For additional support for managing your classroom, see the *Reading Street* Practice Stations' *Classroom Management Handbook*.

USING THE LEVELED READER TEACHING GUIDE

The *Leveled Reader Teaching Guide* provides an instruction plan for each leveled reader based on the same instructional routine.

INTRODUCE THE BOOK The Introduction includes suggestions for creating interest in the text by discussing the title and author, building background, and previewing the book and its features.

READ THE BOOK Before children begin reading the book, have them set purposes for reading and discuss how they can use the reading strategy as they read. Determine how you want children in a particular group to read the text—softly or silently, to a specific point, or the entire text. Then use the Comprehension Questions to provide support as needed and to assess comprehension.

REVISIT THE BOOK The Think and Share questions provide opportunities for children to demonstrate their understanding of the text, the target comprehension skill, and vocabulary. The Response Options require children to revisit the text to respond to what they've read and to move beyond the text to explore related content.

SKILL WORK The Skill Work box provides instruction and practice for the target skill and strategy and selection vocabulary. Instruction for an alternate comprehension skill allows teachers to provide additional skill instruction and practice for children.

USING THE GRAPHIC ORGANIZERS

Graphic organizers in blackline-master format can be found on pages 132–153. These can be used as overhead transparencies or as worksheets.

ASSESSING PERFORMANCE

Use the assessment forms that begin on page 6 to make notes about your children's reading skills, use of reading strategies, and general reading behaviors.

MEASURE FLUENT READING (pp. 6–7) Provides directions for measuring a child's fluency, based on words correct per minute (wcpm), and reading accuracy using a running record.

OBSERVATION CHECKLIST (p. 8) Allows you to note the regularity with which children demonstrate their understanding and use of reading skills and strategies.

READING BEHAVIORS CHECKLIST (p. 9) Provides criteria for monitoring certain reading behaviors.

READING STRATEGY ASSESSMENT (p. 10) Provides criteria for evaluating each child's proficiency as a strategic reader.

PROGRESS REPORT (p. 11) Provides a means to track a child's book-reading progress over a period of time by noting the level at which a child reads and his or her accuracy at that level. Reading the chart from left to right gives you a visual model of how quickly a child is making the transition from one level to the next. Share these reports with parents or guardians to help them see how their child's reading is progressing.

Measure
Fluent Reading

Taking a Running Record

A running record is an assessment of a child's oral reading accuracy and oral reading fluency. Reading accuracy is based on the number of words read correctly. Reading fluency is based on the reading rate (the number of words correct per minute) and the degree to which a child reads with a "natural flow."

How to Measure Reading Accuracy

1. Choose a grade-level text of about 80 to 120 words that is unfamiliar to the child.
2. Make a copy of the text for yourself. Make a copy for the child or have the child read aloud from a book.
3. Give the child the text and have the child read aloud. (You may wish to record the child's reading for later evaluation.)
4. On your copy of the text, mark any miscues or errors the child makes while reading. See the running record sample on page 7, which shows how to identify and mark miscues.
5. Count the total number of words in the text and the total number of errors made by the child. Note: If a child makes the same error more than once, such as mispronouncing the same word multiple times, count it as one error. Self-corrections do not count as actual errors. Use the following formula to calculate the percentage score, or accuracy rate:

$$\frac{\text{Total Number of Words} - \text{Total Number of Errors}}{\text{Total Number of Words}} \times 100 = \text{percentage score}$$

Interpreting the Results

- A child who reads **95–100%** of the words correctly is reading at an **independent level** and may need more challenging text.
- A child who reads **90–94%** of the words correctly is reading at an **instructional level** and will likely benefit from guided instruction.
- A child who reads **89%** or fewer of the words correctly is reading at a **frustrational level** and may benefit most from targeted instruction with lower-level texts and intervention.

How to Measure Reading Rate (WCPM)

1. Follow Steps 1–3 above.
2. Note the exact times when the child begins and finishes reading.
3. Use the following formula to calculate the number of words correct per minute (WCPM):

$$\frac{\text{Total Number of Words Read Correctly}}{\text{Total Number of Seconds}} \times 60 = \text{words correct per minute}$$

Interpreting the Results

By the end of the year, a first-grader should be reading approximately 45–60 WCPM.

Running Record Sample

Running Record Sample

Beth and her friends were eating   6

(lunch) in the park.   10

"Tell us about your trip to the   17
beach," Beth said to one of her friends.   25

"It was great! /grēt/" her friend said.   31

Beth's friends talked about sports,   36
and they talked about movies. But Beth   43
was not talking. *and* She was looking away.   50

"Beth?" they called to her.   55

Beth did not speak. She was looking   62
at bird. It had landed on a sign. Beth   71
just stared. (SC)   73

"I have a feeling," Beth said at last.   81

"What does that mean?" her friends   87
asked.   88

Beth took out her drawing *H* pad. "I   95
need to draw that bird, "~~she~~ *Beth* said.   102

Notations

Accurate Reading
The child reads a word correctly.

Omission
The child omits words or word parts.

Mispronunciation/Misreading
The child pronounces or reads a word incorrectly.

Insertion
The child inserts words or parts of words that are not in the text.

Self-correction
The child reads a word incorrectly but then corrects the error. Do not count self-corrections as actual errors. However, noting self-corrections will help you identify words the child finds difficult.

Hesitation
The child hesitates over a word, and the teacher provides the word. Wait several seconds before telling the child what the word is.

Substitution
The child substitutes words or parts of words for the words in the text.

Running Record Results
Total Number of Words: **102**
Number of Errors: **5**

Reading Time: **136 seconds**

▶ **Reading Accuracy**
$$\frac{102 - 5}{102} \times 100 = 95.098 = 95\%$$

Accuracy Percentage Score: **95%**

▶ **Reading Rate—WCPM**
$$\frac{97}{136} \times 60 = 42.794 = 43 \text{ words correct per minute}$$

Reading Rate: **43 WCPM**

Observation Checklist

Child's Name _____ Date _____

Behaviors Observed	Always (Proficient)	Usually (Fluent)	Sometimes (Developing)	Rarely (Novice)
Reading Strategies and Skills				
Uses prior knowledge and preview to understand what book is about				
Makes predictions and checks them while reading				
Uses context clues to figure out meanings of new words				
Uses phonics and syllabication to decode words				
Self-corrects while reading				
Reads at an appropriate reading rate				
Reads with appropriate intonation and stress				
Uses fix-up strategies				
Identifies story elements: character, setting, plot, theme				
Summarizes plot or main ideas accurately				
Uses target comprehension skill to understand the text better				
Responds thoughtfully about the text				

Behaviors Observed	Always (Proficient)	Usually (Fluent)	Sometimes (Developing)	Rarely (Novice)
Reading Behaviors and Attitudes				
Enjoys listening to stories				
Chooses reading as a free-time activity				
Reads with sustained interest and attention				
Participates in discussion about books				

General Comments

Reading Behaviors Checklist

Child's Name   **Date**

Behavior	Yes	No	Not Applicable
Recognizes letters of the alphabet			
Recognizes name in print			
Recognizes some environmental print, such as signs and logos			
Knows the difference between letters and words			
Knows the difference between capital and lowercase letters			
Understands function of capitalization and punctuation			
Recognizes that book parts, such as the cover, title page, and table of contents, offer information			
Recognizes that words are represented in writing by specific sequences of letters			
Recognizes words that rhyme			
Distinguishes rhyming and nonrhyming words			
Knows letter-sound correspondences			
Identifies and isolates initial sounds in words			
Identifies and isolates final sounds in words			
Blends sounds to make spoken words			
Segments one-syllable spoken words into individual phonemes			
Reads consonant blends and digraphs			
Reads and understands endings, such as -es, -ed, -ing			
Reads vowels and vowel diphthongs			
Reads and understands possessives			
Reads and understands compound words			
Reads simple sentences			
Reads simple stories			
Understands simple story structure			
Other:			

Reading Strategy Assessment

Child _____ Date _____

Teacher _____

		Proficient	Developing	Emerging	Not showing trait
Building Background Comments:	Previews	☐	☐	☐	☐
	Asks questions	☐	☐	☐	☐
	Predicts	☐	☐	☐	☐
	Activates prior knowledge	☐	☐	☐	☐
	Sets own purposes for reading	☐	☐	☐	☐
	Other:	☐	☐	☐	☐
Comprehension Comments:	Retells/summarizes	☐	☐	☐	☐
	Questions, evaluates ideas	☐	☐	☐	☐
	Relates to self/other texts	☐	☐	☐	☐
	Paraphrases	☐	☐	☐	☐
	Rereads/reads ahead for meaning	☐	☐	☐	☐
	Visualizes	☐	☐	☐	☐
	Uses decoding strategies	☐	☐	☐	☐
	Uses vocabulary strategies	☐	☐	☐	☐
	Understands key ideas of a text	☐	☐	☐	☐
	Other:	☐	☐	☐	☐
Fluency Comments:	Adjusts reading rate	☐	☐	☐	☐
	Reads for accuracy	☐	☐	☐	☐
	Uses expression	☐	☐	☐	☐
	Other:	☐	☐	☐	☐
Connections Comments:	Relates text to self	☐	☐	☐	☐
	Relates text to text	☐	☐	☐	☐
	Relates text to world	☐	☐	☐	☐
	Other:	☐	☐	☐	☐
Self-Assessment Comments:	Is aware of: Strengths	☐	☐	☐	☐
	Needs	☐	☐	☐	☐
	Improvement/achievement	☐	☐	☐	☐
	Sets and implements learning goals	☐	☐	☐	☐
	Maintains logs, records, portfolio	☐	☐	☐	☐
	Works with others	☐	☐	☐	☐
	Shares ideas and materials	☐	☐	☐	☐
	Other:	☐	☐	☐	☐

Progress Report

Child's Name _____

At the top of the chart, record the book title, its grade/unit/week (for example, 1.2.3), and the child's accuracy percentage. See page 6 for measuring fluency, calculating accuracy and reading rates. At the bottom of the chart, record the date you took the running record. In the middle of the chart, make an X in the box across from the level of the child's reading—frustrational level (below 89% accuracy), instructional level (90–94% accuracy), or independent level (95–100% accuracy). Record the reading rate (WCPM) in the next row.

Book Title						
Grade/Unit/Week						
Reading Accuracy Percentage						
LEVEL — **Frustrational** (89% or below)						
Instructional (90–94%)						
Independent (95% or above)						
Reading Rate (WCPM)						
Date						

Mack and Zack

SUMMARY A boy named Zack is devoted to Mack, his pet cat, in this simple story.

LESSON VOCABULARY

come	in
my	on
way	

INTRODUCE THE BOOK

INTRODUCE THE TITLE AND AUTHOR Discuss with children the author and title of *Mack and Zack*. Talk about the roles of the author, Ann Rossi, and the illustrator, Chi Chung. Point out the cat on the cover and encourage children to predict what Mack might do in the story. Ask children which part of the book they think came first: the words or the pictures. Remind them to give reasons for their answers.

BUILD BACKGROUND Invite children to share what they know about cats. If any of the children have cats at home, ask them to talk about their pets. If children have read or heard other stories about cats, encourage them to talk about this.

PREVIEW/TAKE A PICTURE WALK Invite children to take a picture walk to preview the text and illustrations. Have children read the text on the title page and compare it to the text on the cover. Explain that the title of the book and names of the author and illustrator always appear on this page. On page 3, point out Zack, the boy, and Mack, the little cat. Ask children to describe what the cat is doing on pages 4 and 5. Focus children's attention on the mat on page 5. Ask: Why would a cat sleep on a mat? Turn to pages 6 and 7 and ask children if they have ever had a cat rub up against them. Have children predict how the story might end, based on the illustration on page 7.

READ THE BOOK

SET PURPOSE Help children set a purpose for reading *Mack and Zack*. Model how to set a purpose: "It looks like this is a story about a boy and his pet cat. I have a pet cat too, so I want to see what happens." Suggest that children think about what they want to learn about the character Zack as they set a purpose for reading.

STRATEGY SUPPORT: MONITOR AND CLARIFY Give children frequent opportunities to read in pairs and small groups. Model thinking aloud and encourage children to think aloud and to ask their classmates questions about the characters, plot, or illustrations as they read. Model questioning: "I wonder what this picture is. Can you tell?"

COMPREHENSION QUESTIONS

PAGE 4 What is Mack eating for a snack? How could you find out what cats eat? *(Possible response: Mack is eating cat food. I could read in a book or ask someone who owns a cat.)*

PAGE 4 Find two rhyming words on this page. Name some other words that rhyme with –*ack*. *(Mack, snack; Reponses will vary.)*

PAGE 6 How would you describe Zack, seeing how he treats Mack? Would you like Zack for a friend? *(Responses will vary but should reflect an understanding of the text.)*

PAGE 7 What part of the book did you like best? Why? *(Responses will vary.)*

REVISIT THE BOOK

THINK AND SHARE

1. Possible responses: care, feed, pet, hold
2. Mack naps on a mat on page 5.
3. Both names have a short *a* and final *ck*.
4. Possible response: *Mack sleeps on Zack's lap.*

EXTEND UNDERSTANDING After children have read the book, lead a discussion about the illustrations. Ask volunteers to point out their favorite illustration. Ask: Did the illustrations help you read? How would you have drawn Zack and his cat? Is there anything you would do differently?

RESPONSE OPTIONS

WRITING Ask children to imagine one more way that Zack can care for his cat. Have them write and illustrate a sentence, using the pattern *Zack can ___*. Remind them to begin each sentence with a capital letter and end it with a period.

SCIENCE CONNECTION

TIME FOR Science

Provide children with a few nonfiction books about cats and their care. Suggest that children consult the books to find three facts about cat care. Encourage them to share their discoveries with their classmates.

Skill Work

TEACH/REVIEW VOCABULARY

Write the words *come*, *my*, and *way* on the board. Read the words aloud as a group and practice spelling them. Give children a copy of a newspaper or magazine article and have them circle the examples of *come*, *my*, and *way* they find.

TARGET SKILL AND STRATEGY

CHARACTER AND SETTING Remind children that *characters* are people or animals in stories. Characters can be real, or they can be made up. In *Mack and Zack*, the main characters are a boy named Zack and his cat, Mack. Remind children that when they read, they should think about what the characters in a story do and how they feel. They can look for clues in the words and pictures. Ask: On page 3, how do you think Zack is feeling as he holds the cat? How can you tell? Discuss the smile on Zack's face and how it reveals his affection for the cat. The *setting* is where a story takes place. Point out the details in the illustrations that show Zack and Mack appear to be in their home.

MONITOR AND CLARIFY Point out to children that good readers ask themselves questions as they read or *monitor*. They make sure they understand what the characters are doing. Discuss how, when they have questions they can't answer, they can ask for help from their classmates and teachers and *clarify*.

ADDITIONAL SKILL INSTRUCTION

MAIN IDEA Ask children to think about what the story *Mack and Zack* was about. Help children see that sometimes the title of a story tells them what a story is about. Other times, they may need to think about what they read and use their own words to tell what the story is about.

ELL Have children write the sentence *Come my way* in both English and their home language. Then have them draw a picture to go along with the sentences.

Name _____

Character and Setting

1. Draw one way that Zack takes care of his cat Mack.

Draw Zack and Mack's house.

2. Finish the sentence.

Zack thinks Mack is _____ .

Name _____

Vocabulary

Read each sentence and the words above it. Write the correct word on the line to finish the sentence.

come   from   play

_____

1. Call Mack and he will _____ .

say   wag   way

_____

2. Which _____ did Mack go?

in   my   he

_____

3. Mack is hiding _____ my closet.

he   on   my

_____

4. Mack is _____ the mat.

my   she   it

_____

5. I hold Mack in _____ arms.

The Sick Pets

SUMMARY In this story, three sick dogs are at a vet's office, where the vet cares for them. The story supports the lesson concept that people help animals.

LESSON VOCABULARY

she	take
up	what

INTRODUCE THE BOOK

INTRODUCE THE TITLE AND AUTHOR Discuss with children the title and author of *The Sick Pets*. Also have children look at the picture on the cover. Tell children that social studies includes learning about why people work at a job. Ask: How might this story have something to do with social studies?

BUILD BACKGROUND Ask: What should you do if you have a pet that is sick? After children have answered, have them share what they know about animal doctors.

PREVIEW Have children preview by looking at the pictures in the book. Ask: Where does this story mostly take place? Have children read the heading on page 8. Ask: Is this page part of the story? Look at the photo. Why do you think this page is in the book?

READ THE BOOK

SET PURPOSE Have children set a purpose for reading *The Sick Pets*. Ask children to think about what they noticed in their preview. Ask: What do you want to find out by reading this story?

STRATEGY SUPPORT: SUMMARIZE Remind children that good readers are able to use their own words to tell the important things that happen in a book or what the book is about. Using their own words to retell is a way of showing that they have understood what they have read. Model page 5: "On this page, I read that the man is Tim and his dog is named Vin. Tim is picking Vin up from the vet's office. To tell what happens in my own words, I ask, 'What is this page mostly about?' I will use my own words to tell: "Tim's dog, Vin, was sick. But now Tim can take him home." As children read *The Sick Pets*, have them tell the main idea of each page by asking" What is this page mostly about?

COMPREHENSION QUESTIONS

PAGE 5 The dog, Pip, is sick. Could that really happen, or is it make-believe" Why? *(Possible response: It could really happen, because animals can get sick.)*

PAGE 6 What did the vet do? *(She listened to Pip's heartbeat.)*

PAGE 7 Who was TIm? *(He was Vin's owner.)*

REVISIT THE BOOK

THINK AND SHARE

1. They all got better.
2. Vets can help sick animals get well.
3. *fix, Bix*
4. Possible responses: What tools do you use? Was it hard learning to be a vet?

EXTEND UNDERSTANDING Have children explore the plot of *The Sick Pets*. Give them a sequence graphic organizer. Have them fill in what happens first, next, and last in the story.

RESPONSE OPTIONS

WRITING Have children compare characters. Tell them to write three words that describe Pip and three words that describe Vin.

SOCIAL STUDIES CONNECTION

Time For
SOCIAL
STUDIES

Display books and other information about different kinds of doctors, such as vets, pediatricians, optometrists, dentists, and cardiologists. Have children complete this sentence for each kind of doctor: *A (kind of doctor) takes care of* _____.

Skill Work

TEACH/REVIEW VOCABULARY

Give children sets of vocabulary word cards. Write these sentences on the chalkboard: *Please ____ me to the zoo. I like it ____ . ____ do you have? ____ is here.* Read each sentence aloud and have children show the word that fits best.

ELL Give children vocabulary word cards. Challenge them to go on a classroom scavenger hunt to find the words in environmental print.

TARGET SKILL AND STRATEGY

PLOT Write on the chalkboard: *Pip, Bix, and Vin are sick.* Tell children that these are the first things we learn in this story. Have children turn to page 6 and summarize the next event. *(The vet fixes Pip, Bix, and Vin.)* Explain that these events are part of the *plot*, or what happens in a story. A story's plot has a beginning, middle, and end. Ask: How does this story end? *(Tim takes Vin back.)*

SUMMARIZE Remind children that good readers are able to tell what a book is about in their own words. If they can use their own words to tell what the book is mostly about, it helps them tell whether a story could really happen or is make-believe.

ADDITIONAL SKILL INSTRUCTION

DRAW CONCLUSIONS Tell children that they can use what they read and see and what they know about real life to figure out more about what happens in the story. Model: On page 6, it looks like the vet is using a stethoscope to listen to Pip's heartbeat. I know that my doctor listens to my heartbeat and breathing when I am sick. Based on what I read and what I know, I think the vet is checking Pip to help Pip get better.

Name _____

Plot

Read the story. Use the boxes to draw a picture of what happens in the beginning, middle, and end.

> Rabbit loves gardens. Rabbit hops into the garden.
>
> Rabbit sees a carrot. Rabbit eats the carrot.
>
> Rabbit sees a dog. Rabbit hops out of the garden.

Beginning

Middle

End

18

Name _____

Vocabulary

Look at the words in the box. Find the words in the puzzle.
Circle the words.

Words to Know

she	take	up	what

```
c  b  a  n  d  e  w
x  d  f  l  g  o  h
s  u  p  n  i  q  a
h  a  t  a  k  e  t
e  i  y  v  b  i  w
```

Where They Live

SUMMARY Tom likes the country and Pam prefers the city. In the end, they discover a solution that satisfies them both.

LESSON VOCABULARY

blue	from	get
help	little	use

INTRODUCE THE BOOK

INTRODUCE THE TITLE AND AUTHOR Discuss with children the title and author of *Where They Live*. Point out the characters on the cover illustration and ask children to predict what might happen in the story, based on what they see. Ask: Does the girl look happy? How can you tell? Turn to the title page and read the names of the author and illustrator. Discuss their roles.

BUILD BACKGROUND Invite children to share what they know about the differences between city life and country life. Encourage them to recall stories they have already read or heard on this topic, such as "The Country Mouse and the City Mouse." Ask children to think of words that describe each setting. List the children's ideas in a two-column chart.

PREVIEW/TAKE A PICTURE WALK Lead children on a picture walk through the book. Point out Tom's expression on page 4 and Pam's expression on page 6. Ask children what Tom and Pam might be feeling in these pictures. Have children describe the pictures on page 7 and predict how the story might end.

READ THE BOOK

SET PURPOSE Have children set a purpose for reading *Where They Live*. Suggest that they recall the questions and observations that arose when they previewed the illustrations. Model how to set a purpose: I think that Pam does not look happy on the cover. I'm going to read and find out if I'm right.

STRATEGY SUPPORT: VISUALIZE Visualizing events helps children understand and remember what they are reading. As children read *Where They Live*, encourage them to pause after each page and picture the events in their minds. Model visualizing on page 3: When I read that Tom and Tip live on a farm, I picture in my mind what that farm is like. I see lots of animals, such as chickens, pigs, and horses. I also see people working hard on the farm.

COMPREHENSION QUESTIONS

PAGE 3 Where are Tom and Tip? How do you think Tom feels about the farm? (*Possible responses: Tom and Tip are on the farm; Tom is smiling.*)

PAGE 4 What might Tom be thinking? What does that tell you about Tom? (*Possible response: Tom might be thinking, "I want to go back to the farm." He doesn't like the city.*)

PAGE 5 Where might Pam and Mops go in a cab? (*Possible response: They might go to visit Tom and Tip.*)

PAGE 6 Will Pam and Mops go back to town? Why do you think so? (*Yes, because Tom and Tip went back to the farm from town.*)

PAGE 7 Did you like the ending of the story? Why or why not? (*Responses will vary according to personal preference.*)

REVISIT THE BOOK

THINK AND SHARE

1. Tom, Tip
2. Possible response: I pictured both characters to be very happy. This helped me understand why they like their own homes.
3. Responses will vary, but should demonstrate understanding of the word *help*. Possible response: The characters are afraid of places they do not like.
4. Possible response: The characters will get upset.

EXTEND UNDERSTANDING Return to the chart on country and city life that children generated before reading *Where They Live*. Invite them to revise the list, adding the new information they learned by reading. Ask children to tell whether they would prefer to live in the country or in the city and explain why.

RESPONSE OPTIONS

WRITING As a group, brainstorm other ways the story could have ended. Invite children to illustrate an alternate ending to the story and write a few sentences about their pictures.

DRAMA CONNECTION Suggest that children dramatize *Where They Live*. Let children choose characters and act out the story as a narrator reads it aloud. Encourage children to make up dialogue for their characters.

Skill Work

TEACH/REVIEW VOCABULARY

List the vocabulary words on the board. Have children find the words in the text and read the sentences in which they are found. Then write the words on index cards. Let children take turns picking a card, reading the word, and using it in a sentence.

ELL Play a guessing game with English language learners. Let each child select a word card and act out the word for the others in the group to guess.

TARGET SKILL AND STRATEGY

CHARACTER AND SETTING Point out that *characters* are the people or animals in stories. Characters can be real, or they can be made up. When good readers read a story, they think about what the characters say and do, and they also think about when and where the story happens. As children read *Where They Live*, discuss the characters' feelings and actions. Ask: What does Tom like to do? What does Pam think about the farm? Have children describe the *setting* of each scene. Encourage them to support their ideas with details from the text or illustrations.

VISUALIZE As children read, ask them to picture the story events and settings in their mind. Say: When you picture events in your mind, you can understand more about the story. Have children turn to page 4 and ask them to visualize what a busy city must look like to someone who is not use to it. Ask: How does this help you understand the story better? (*Possible response: It helps me see why Tim and Tip like the farm better.*)

ADDITIONAL SKILL INSTRUCTION

THEME AND PLOT Point out to children that by thinking about the story and using information from their lives, readers can figure out the "big idea" of a story. Stories also have a beginning, middle, and end—main events that form the *plot*. As a group, develop a story map that shows the beginning, middle, and ending events in *Where They Live*. Ask: What do you think the author wanted you to learn by reading this story?

Name _____

Character and Setting

Think about the **characters** in the story.
Think about **setting** or where the story takes place.
Then make drawings.

I. Draw where Tom and Tip like to be. Show how Tom and Tip feel.

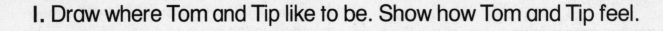

2. Draw where Pam and Mops like to be. Show how Pam and Mops feel.

Name _____

Vocabulary

Unscramble the words to finish each sentence.

_____
- -
1. mrof _____   Pam and Mops come _____ the town.

_____
- -
2. etg _____   They will _____ in a cab.

_____
- -
3. pleh _____   _____! There are too many cars here!

4. Circle the words that sound like **blue**.

   Sue   tub   glue

5. Circle the word that has a vowel that says its name.

   little   help   use

6. Circle the word that has a double consonant.

   use   help   little

Which Fox?

SUMMARY This nonfiction selection contrasts two foxes, one in the wild and one in a zoo. The book shows how wild animals adapt to their environments.

LESSON VOCABULARY

eat	five	four
her	this	too

INTRODUCE THE BOOK

INTRODUCE THE TITLE AND AUTHOR Discuss with students the title and the author of *Which Fox?* Based on the title, ask if anyone has ever seen a fox, and if so, where. Guide children to see that a fox looks like a medium-sized dog. Ask them to predict what this book is about.

BUILD BACKGROUND Have children name animals they know. Point out that animals living in the forest or jungle are wild, and animals living in homes are tame. Encourage use of the words *wild* and *tame* as children discuss the animals named earlier. Then, discuss how animals in a zoo are not entirely wild nor are they tame. Help children understand that animals adapt to their environment.

PREVIEW/TAKE A PICTURE WALK Have children preview the pictures. Children may need help identifying which fox is being discussed on a given page. Point out details in the art that clarify the fox being discussed as well as the use of the comparison word *too*. Discuss content that may not be familiar to children, such as a den and a zookeeper who feeds animals.

READ THE BOOK

SET PURPOSE Tell the children to set a purpose for reading this book. Have them think about how they like animals, if they have favorite animals they see at the zoo, or whether they have noticed how animals get used to living in different areas.

STRATEGY SUPPORT: IMPORTANT IDEAS Tell children that a story is full of many ideas. Some ideas are more important than others. Important ideas tell more about the main idea of the book. Encourage children to look for important ideas as they read.

COMPREHENSION QUESTIONS

PAGE 3 What does a fox living in the woods eat? *(small animals)*

PAGES 4–5 Why is it easy to watch a fox in the zoo and not easy to watch a fox in the wild? *(The fox in the zoo stays in one area; the fox in the wild will chase animals anywhere.)*

PAGE 7 What does a fox in a zoo do to get dinner? *(It waits for a worker to feed it.)*

REVISIT THE BOOK

THINK AND SHARE

1. Two foxes living in different places get food and do things differently.
2. Possible response: Foxes can live in the woods or in a zoo. This helped me see why they are different.
3. There is more than one animal in the story.
4. Zoo fox: She is fed by a zookeeper.
   Woods fox: She looks for her dinner herself.
   Both: They both eat meat.

EXTEND UNDERSTANDING Help the children to understand that they can help themselves to find the main idea by looking at the pictures and talking about what is happening. Have children practice reading pages of the book aloud on their own or in pairs. Then, ask them about the details so that together the children begin to see that the one main idea has to do with where the animals live.

RESPONSE OPTIONS

WRITING Have children describe how the two foxes are the same and different. Suggest they use words that tell about what is alike, such as *also* and *too*. Then, discuss words that show differences, such as *but* and *or*. Ask children to think about which fox they would prefer to be and why.

ELL Make a word web to help children organize facts they already know about foxes. Ask: What is a fox? What does it look like? Where do foxes live? What do foxes eat? Prompt students to answer questions with *yes* or *no*. Record new facts children learn after reading.

SCIENCE CONNECTION

TIME FOR Science

Children can share information about foxes that was presented in the book. Encourage them to ask questions of one another. Continue adding to the Venn diagram that you began earlier. Have children compare how the foxes are alike and how they are different.

Skill Work

TEACH/REVIEW VOCABULARY

Most of the high-frequency words will be familiar to children—*eat, her, this, too*. Define all other new words contextually using the illustrations. You may want to have the content words—*fox, hunts, animals, den, dinner, watch*—written on index cards for students to work in pairs to learn.

TARGET SKILL AND STRATEGY

MAIN IDEA AND DETAILS Explain to children that the *main idea* tells what a book or paragraph is mostly about. To help children identify the main idea as they read, encourage them to:

• Ask themselves what each page or the whole selection is about.

• Think of one sentence that explains the most important point the author is making.

• Look for clues about major ideas in the title and pictures.

IMPORTANT IDEAS Explain to children that *important ideas* tell more about the main idea. Some ideas are more important than others. Have children read page 4, and ask: What is an important idea on this page? (*The fox is in the zoo.*)

ADDITIONAL SKILL INSTRUCTION

COMPARE AND CONTRAST Remind students that they will often use the skill of finding what is *alike* and what is *different* to understand their reading. Make a T-chart on the board listing the qualities of the two kinds of foxes. Fill in the list together. Then ask the children: How are the two foxes alike? How are they different?

Name _____

Main Idea and Details

Read each part of *Which Fox?*
Find the big idea.
Circle the correct answer.

This is a fox.
She eats little animals.
She is in the woods.

1. What are the sentences about?
   animals   eating   a fox in the woods

This is a fox too.
She is in the zoo.
We like watching her.

2. What are the sentences about?
   watching   a fox in the zoo   zoo

Circle the answer to finish each sentence.
Write it on the line.

3. The fox in the woods has to _____ for dinner.
   look   sit   fix

4. The fox in the zoo _____ dinner.
   hunts   gets   does not have

Name _____

Vocabulary

Draw a line from each word in the first column to the same word in the second column.

1. eat

heat
feet
eat

2. four

for
four
fort

3. this

that
miss
this

4. too

to
too
two

5. Write each word on the line.

eat _____

her _____

this _____

five _____

What Animals Can You See?

SUMMARY Fran and her parents take a walk to look for animals. They see a frog, a bird, and a deer. Each is in its own habitat, and each is eating. The illustrations show each animal's habitat along with the joy Fran's family is having on this walk. At the end of the walk, Fran wants to eat her own dinner.

LESSON VOCABULARY

saw	small
tree	your

INTRODUCE THE BOOK

INTRODUCE THE TITLE AND AUTHOR Discuss with students the title and the author of *What Animals Can You See?* Based on the title, ask the children to predict what they will see. Ask if they think this will be a make-believe story or a story that could really happen.

BUILD BACKGROUND It's important to set the stage for the children to think about the animals that live around us and we see every day. If you have a class pet, put the pet in a central place, or if there are children's drawings of everyday animals, put them up. With some props in the classroom setting, ask the children to guess what the story will be about. Help them to distinguish between animals in the wild and the ones we see every day as pets.

PREVIEW Invite children to page through the book, looking at the pictures. Ask what they notice about animals in the story. Draw attention to the beginning and ending illustrations and ask how they are alike. *(The family goes out to walk and comes back home.)*

READ THE BOOK

SET PURPOSE Have students set a purpose for reading *What Animals Can You See?* Students are easily interested in animals, so talk about animals they saw at home or on the way to school today. Ask them to imagine what animal they might like to pretend to be. Perhaps they would like to be one of the animals Fran sees in this book.

STRATEGY SUPPORT: STORY STRUCTURE Tell children that stories are arranged in order from beginning to end. After reading *What Animals Can You See?*, have children retell the story in their own words. Encourage them to tell what happens in the beginning, middle, and end.

COMPREHENSION QUESTIONS

PAGE 3 Who is Fran and what did she go out to see? *(Fran is the girl in the story who goes for a walk with her family to see real animals.)*

PAGES 4–6 What were all the animals doing? *(They were all eating in their habitats.)*

PAGE 7 What do both people and animals need to do? *(They both eat.)*

PAGE 8 Birds leave their nests when they grow up. How is this like anything humans do? *(Children, like birds, grow up and leave home.)*

ELL Ask the children to draw an animal they often see, and ask them to mention one or more of the names the animal may have. Begin a discussion of how everyday animals may be different in different places.

REVIST THE BOOK

THINK AND SHARE

1. Responses will vary, but should relate to the story content.
2. Possible responses: They see a frog eating in a log, a bird eating in a nest, and a deer eating in the woods.
3. a; F, r, n.
4. Possible response: any animals found in a woods near a residential area such as mice, squirrels, etc.

EXTEND UNDERSTANDING Experiment with this simple way of telling a story in a progression that includes simple facts about animals. To help the children learn how to tell such a story, make up a spoken story with the class. Use a couple of volunteers to be the human characters and some to be the animal characters. Have the students suggest events that could make up a plot. Help the students to bring the story to an end by thinking up a twist, in which a human learns a lesson from an animal, or offering a funny ending.

RESPONSE OPTIONS

SPEAKING Suggest that the children make up their own story about animals they saw on the way to school. Remind them that the animals can be small, even tiny insects if they choose. Also, suggest that the animals be doing something that the children have seen animals do in real life.

SCIENCE CONNECTION

Suggest that the children make up animal "riddle pictures." After discussing animals the children have seen, have them draw two environments where animals live. They should draw the environments with as much detail as they want but they should not show the animal. Then have them draw the correct animal on the back of each environment. Hang the pictures and have a contest to guess which animal lives in each home.

Skill Work

TEACH/REVIEW VOCABULARY

Most of the high-frequency words will be familiar to children — *saw, small, tree, your*. Define all other new words contextually using the illustrations. You may want to have the content words — *look, woods, animals, dinner* — written on index cards for students to work in pairs to learn.

TARGET SKILL AND STRATEGY

MAIN IDEA AND DETAILS Tell children that a *main* idea is what a story is all about. Guide students in identifying the main idea of *What Animals Can You See?* by asking: In the beginning of the story, what does Fran want to look at on her family's walk? What does the family see while they are walking? Did Fran get to see what she wanted to see?

STORY STRUCTURE Remind children that each event that happens in a story leads to another event. This makes up the beginning, middle, and end of a story. Recall well-known stories with children, such as the story of Cinderella, and help them determine what happens in the beginning, middle, and end of the story.

ADDITIONAL SKILL INSTRUCTION

COMPARE AND CONTRAST Discuss likenesses and differences to teach the skill *compare and contrast*. For instance, make a T-chart on the board with one column for the animals and one for Fran's family. Have the children tell you what characteristics to write in each column. Together discuss the likenesses and differences between animals and humans.

Name _____

Main Idea and Details

Read each question and the answer choices below it.
Circle the right answer.

1. What is *What Animals Can You See?* mostly about?

   a. birds in a nest

   b. a girl looking at animals

   c. a deer eating dinner

2. What is the most important idea about Fran?

   a. She is hungry.

   b. She has a mom and a dad.

   c. She enjoys looking at animals.

Read these sentences. Then answer the question below it.

> A frog is eating dinner in a log. Small birds are
> eating dinner in a nest. A deer is eating dinner in
> the woods. Fran is going to eat dinner at home.
> Animals and people eat dinner.

3. What are the sentences all about?

   a. eating dinner

   b. taking walks

   c. eating breakfast

30

Name _____

Vocabulary

Words to Know
saw   small   tree   your

Choose the word from the box that best completes each sentence. Then write it on the line.

_____

----

1. The deer is eating leaves from a _____ .

_____

----

2. The baby birds are _____ .

_____

----

3. Fran _____ trees and birds in the park.

_____

----

4. Fran and her family live in a house like _____ family does.

5. Draw a picture to show what is happening in the sentence.

One small bird is leaving the nest.

31

Which Animals Will We See?

◉ **CAUSE AND EFFECT**
◉ **STORY STRUCTURE**

SUMMARY As readers "walk through the forest" shown in this book, they see animals by looking near, far, up, and down. A variety of photographs support readers' comprehension. A special section about ants will spark their interest.

LESSON VOCABULARY

home	into
many	them

INTRODUCE THE BOOK

INTRODUCE THE TITLE AND AUTHOR Discuss the title and the author of *Which Animals Will We See?* Ask children to look at the photograph on the cover and predict where the events of this book will take place. Ask children how the topic of animals relates to science.

BUILD BACKGROUND Discuss with the class the characteristics of forests. Many children will have walked through a forest themselves. Ask: What kinds of trees did you see in the forest? Was the ground that you walked on smooth or rough? What sounds did you hear in a forest? What did you smell in the forest?

ELL Invite children to share the words in their home languages for *forest, tree, ant,* and *bird.* Elicit discussion about the similarities and differences between forests. Ask: What do you think all forests have in common? Do you think there are forests everywhere?

PREVIEW Have children look at the photographs in the book. Encourage them to name the animals that they know. Ask if children have seen any of the animals in other contexts—at a nature preserve, in another book, or even in their own backyards.

READ THE BOOK

SET PURPOSE Guide children to set a purpose for reading by explaining that the book is about animals you might see in the forest. Prompt children to think of an animal that lives in a forest and read to see if that animal is in the book.

STRATEGY SUPPORT: STORY STRUCTURE Tell children that all stories have a beginning, middle, and end. This is called the *story structure.* As they read, have children think about how each event leads to another.

COMPREHENSION QUESTIONS

PAGE 3 How should you walk if you want to see animals in a forest and not scare them away? *(Possible response: You should walk slowly and quietly.)*

PAGE 4 What do you notice about the bird's nest in the picture? *(Possible response: It is big and up high.)*

PAGE 6 In what direction would you look to see this ant? *(down)*

PAGE 8 Why do the worker ants take care of ant eggs and the ant babies? *(because there is only one queen)*

REVISIT THE BOOK

THINK AND SHARE

1. Possible response: because they walked around in a forest
2. Possible response: I could imagine that each page was a new place the family stopped to look at animals.
3. *hunt*
4. Possible response: What do animals do when it rains?

EXTEND UNDERSTANDING After children have read page 3, ask them what the photograph tells them about the people in the story. Ask: Do you think the four people in the photograph are a family? How do you know? Who is the youngest in the photograph? Why are they holding each other's hands? Do you think they are enjoying themselves?

RESPONSE OPTIONS

WRITING Have children write a story three sentences long. Tell them that the first sentence is the beginning, the second sentence is the middle, and the third sentence is the end.

WORD WORK Lead an activity using sentence frames like the following: *A forest is ____. A forest has ____. You can ____ in a forest.*

SCIENCE CONNECTION

Have each child choose an environment in your community such as a marsh, woods, desert, or beach. Provide disposable print materials, like old magazines, for children to look through and find different animals that live in that environment. Have children cut and paste pictures they find on their own papers.

Skill Work

TEACH/REVIEW VOCABULARY

Have children take turns using each vocabulary word in a sentence. Ask children to say their sentences aloud as you record them on the board. Assist children in reading sentences from the board.

TARGET SKILL AND STRATEGY

CAUSE AND EFFECT Lead children to see *cause-and-effect* relationships by asking children to think as they read about things that happen and why they happen. Ask: What happened on page 4? *(They saw birds.)* Why did it happen? *(They looked up.)* Summarize the children's response using the word *because.* Say: They saw birds because they looked up.

STORY STRUCTURE Remind children that the beginning, middle, and end of a story is called the *story structure.* As they read, have children tell what happens at the beginning, middle, and end of *Which Animals Will We See?*

ADDITIONAL SKILL INSTRUCTION

SETTING AND PLOT After children finish reading, ask them to recall where the events of the story took place. Next create a story map together. First fill in information about the setting. Then ask children what happened in the beginning, middle, and end of the book.

Name _____

Cause and Effect

In the story, the family saw animals because they went into a forest. What happened? The family saw animals. Why did it happen? They went into the forest. Complete the sentences below. Draw a line to connect what happened to why it happened.

What happened?   **Why did it happen?**

1. I got wet.   **a.** because it was night

2. I was tired.   **b.** because it rained

3. I ate.   **c.** because I was hungry

4. Write a sentence about something that happened today and why it happened. Hint: use the word *because*.

_____

_____

_____

Name _____

Vocabulary

Pick a word from the box to finish each sentence.
Write it on the line.

| Words to Know |
| home   into   many   them |

1. The fox ran _____ the bushes.

2. Look at the birds building a nest. Can you

   see _____ ?

3. The forest is _____ to some animals.

4. There are _____ ants on the branch.

5. We saw a lot. Let's go _____ .

35

Let's Go to the Zoo

SUMMARY A boy and his mother visit the zoo and see all kinds of animals.

LESSON VOCABULARY

catch	good
no	put
said	want

INTRODUCE THE BOOK

INTRODUCE THE TITLE AND AUTHOR Discuss the title and author of *Let's Go to the Zoo*. Have children discuss what the book might be about. Ask: Who do you think is going to go to the zoo? How do the title and cover help you know what the book will be about?

BUILD BACKGROUND Ask children to discuss their own experiences of visiting a zoo. Ask: Whom did you go to the zoo with? What animals did you see? What was your favorite part of the zoo? If some children have not been to a zoo, discuss what they would like to see if they did go to a zoo.

PREVIEW/TAKE A PICTURE WALK Invite children to take a picture walk to preview the text and pictures. Ask them to identify the different animals they see. Discuss what they think might happen in the book.

ELL Provide a web for children. In the center of the web, write the word zoo. Then have them write examples of different animals and objects they might see at a zoo, such as different kinds of animals, zoo workers, food stands, and so on. Children can also draw the different zoo-related objects or the names of them in their home language next to the English words.

READ THE BOOK

SET PURPOSE Have children set a purpose for reading *Let's Go to the Zoo*. Children's interest in zoos and zoo animals should guide this purpose. Suggest children think about what it is like to visit a zoo.

STRATEGY SUPPORT: PREDICT AND SET PURPOSE Encourage children to use what they already know to make predictions and set a purpose for reading. For example, have children use what they know about zoos to predict what might happen at the zoo in the story. Explain that their purpose for reading may be to find out if their ideas about what might happen are correct.

COMPREHENSION QUESTIONS

PAGE 4 What are the first animals the boy and his mother see at the zoo? Who is playing catch with these animals? *(They see the seals first. A zookeeper is playing catch with the seals.)*

PAGE 5 What animals eat from the boy's hand? *(The goats eat from his hand.)*

PAGE 7 How do you think the boy feels about leaving the zoo? Why? *(Possible response: He is sad, because he wishes they had more time to stay.)*

REVISIT THE BOOK

THINK AND SHARE

1. Seals; goats; bears; giraffes
2. Possible responses: I thought they would see the monkeys first, because they were pointing to the monkey exhibit on the map. I was wrong. They saw the seals first.
3. The word *tall*, on page 7, has the same sound as the word *ball*.
4. Possible response: I would want to see the monkeys, because they are my favorite animal.

EXTEND UNDERSTANDING Invite children to discuss what it is like to visit a zoo. Encourage them to use all of their senses as they describe the experience. Remind them to include other things they might see besides animals, such as zoo workers, balloons, food stands, water, and so on.

RESPONSE OPTIONS

ART Invite children to create their own map of a zoo. Tell them they can include whatever animals they would like to see at a zoo. Remind them to add a title for their map and labels for each of the exhibits.

SCIENCE CONNECTION

Invite children to think about the reasons why we have zoos and why people like to visit zoos. List the reasons on the board. For example, zoos help animals that are in danger and they give people a chance to see and learn about animals they might not otherwise get to see in real life.

Skill Work

TEACH/REVIEW VOCABULARY

Write the vocabulary words on the board where everyone can see them. Going around in a circle, have each child use one of the words in a sentence.

TARGET SKILL AND STRATEGY

SEQUENCE Tell children that a good way to understand what happens in a story is be clear about the order in which events happen. Encourage children to pay attention to the order of events that take place as the boy and his mother visit the zoo animals. Review the graphic organizer at the back of the book. Let children know that they will be making one just like it and filling it in after reading.

PREDICT AND SET PURPOSE Remind children that thinking about what might happen next in a story helps them make sense of what they read. Explain that when they think about what happens next, they should continue to read to see if what they thought was right.

ADDITIONAL SKILL INSTRUCTION

COMPARE AND CONTRAST Have children look at the pictures on pages 4 and 5. Encourage them to describe each set of animals, including where they live and what they do. Ask children to describe how these animals are alike and different.

Name _____

Sequence

Use the boxes below to retell the events from the story. Make sure your pictures are in the order of what happened.

1.

2.

3.

Name _____

Vocabulary

Circle the word that best completes each sentence.
Write the word on the line.

want   catch   good
_____
- -

1. All children _____ to have fun.

want   put   no
_____
- -

2. They tell the barking pup, "_____ !"

said   good   want
_____
- -

3. Dad's new car looks _____ .

catch   no   good
_____
- -

4. The pup will _____ the ball.

said   good   put
_____
- -

5. Grandma will _____ us to bed.

no   said   good
_____
- -

6. My sister _____, "You cannot come in my room."

A Class

SUMMARY *The Class*, a photographic nonfiction book, observes the activities of a group of elementary school children as they participate in activities such as taking care of the class pet, going to the park, and riding the school bus home at the end of the day.

LESSON VOCABULARY

be	could	horse
of	old	paper

INTRODUCE THE BOOK

INTRODUCE THE TITLE AND AUTHOR Discuss with children the title and author of *A Class*. Have children describe what the children on the cover might be doing. Ask them to tell what information they might expect to find in a book called *A Class* and explain why. Then, ask volunteers to read the text on the title page. Have children compare the words on this page to the words on the cover.

BUILD BACKGROUND Invite children to talk about what it means to be a class. Ask: What kinds of things does our class do together? What do other classes do? Record children's ideas on a concept map. After reading the book, review the concept map and invite children to add to or change their ideas.

PREVIEW/TAKE A PICTURE WALK Invite children to preview the photographs on a picture walk. Turn to page 3 and ask children to describe the children in the picture. On page 4, point out the school supplies and ask children to compare the materials in the photo with those in their own classroom. Invite children to predict how the story might end, then have them turn to page 8 and look at the photograph on this page. Have children read the words on the school bus and talk about what the children in the picture are doing.

READ THE BOOK

SET PURPOSE Have children set a purpose for reading *A Class*. Suggest that they think back to the questions that arose as they were previewing the book and each choose one question for which to find an answer.

STRATEGY SUPPORT: MONITOR AND CLARIFY Model thinking aloud and using the photographs to enhance comprehension: I don't understand what the class is looking at. Maybe the pictures will make it clearer. As children read *A Class*, remind them to ask themselves questions about the text and to use the photographs to help answer those questions.

COMPREHENSION QUESTIONS

PAGE 3 How old are the children in this class? How old are you? What do you think they could be doing? *(Possible response: They are six years old and I am too. They could be looking at pictures in a book.)*

PAGE 4 What is happening in this picture? Why is it happening? *(Possible response: The children are drawing, because it is art time.)*

PAGE 5 What do you think the boy does to take care of the class pet? Why do you think so? *(Possible answer: He feeds it and gives it water. That's how we take care of our class pet.)*

PAGE 8 How is this class like your class? How is it different? *(Responses will vary, but should relate to information in the book and children's personal experience.)*

REVISIT THE BOOK

THINK AND SHARE

1. Possible response: It is time to go home.
2. Possible response: There are shelves filled with books and other school supplies.
3. cage
4. Possible response: The animals live on a farm. Cows and chickens could live there too.

EXTEND UNDERSTANDING Support children in comparing their class to the class pictured in the book. Together, fill out a two-column chart with the headings *The Book's Class* and *Our Class*. In the first column, list the activities mentioned in the book. List your class's activities in the second column.

RESPONSE OPTIONS

WRITING The text of *A Class* has two questions for children to answer. Suggest that children choose one question to copy and answer. Encourage them to illustrate their pages.

SOCIAL STUDIES CONNECTION

Time For **SOCIAL STUDIES**

Invite children to imagine that a child who has never been to their school wants to know all about their class. What would they tell this child? Have children collaborate to write and illustrate a book that describes the daily activities in their classroom.

Skill Work

TEACH/REVIEW VOCABULARY

List the vocabulary words on the board. Find each word in the text and read it in context. After discussing each word and its meaning, have children spell the word aloud. Make up a rhythmic chant for each vocabulary word. Then have children write each word in the air as they spell it aloud.

TARGET SKILL AND STRATEGY

CAUSE AND EFFECT Remind children that when good readers read a story, they think about what happened and why it happened. Turn off the lights in the room and discuss what happened *(the room got dark)* and why *(the lights were turned off)*. As children read *A Class*, turn to specific pages and ask children to explain what happened and why.

ELL Have English language learners use a graphic organizer to help identify what happened in the book and why it happened. Use the example on the Think and Share page as a model.

MONITOR AND CLARIFY Point out to children that what they read should make sense. If the words they read are confusing, or they're not sure what is happening and why, it can be helpful to look at the illustrations.

ADDITIONAL SKILL INSTRUCTION

AUTHOR'S PURPOSE Point out to children that *A Class* was written by an author and that the author had a reason for writing. As children preview the book, ask them to find the name of the author and to ask themselves: Why might the author have written this book? As they discuss *A Class* after reading, ask them to think back to their predictions about why the author wrote the selection and see if they have any new ideas. Encourage them to give reasons for their answers.

Name _____

Cause and Effect

Read the sentences.

It was time to go home.
The kids got on the school bus.

Why did it happen?

What happened?

Draw what happened.

Name _____

Vocabulary

Read the clues.
Then use words from the box to fill in the crossword puzzle.

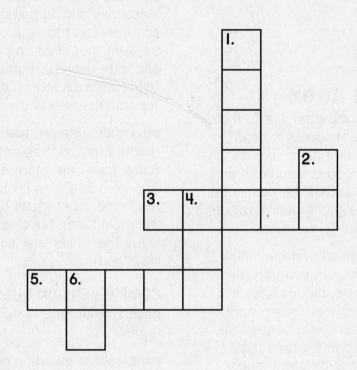

Words to Know

be   could   horse   of   old   paper

Down

1. Drake will put new ___ on the desk.
2. Blake will ___ the pet helper.
4. Max will throw out the ____ crayons.
6. They will take care ____ their pet.

Across

3. Jen will draw a brown _____.
5. What other jobs _____ the kids do?

Look at My Neighborhood

SUMMARY In this book, readers discover the different neighborhoods in which people may live. Some people live in cities with many people, while others live in neighborhoods with many animals in the country. Neighborhoods can have parks to play ball, places to ride bikes, or even a lake for swimming. Readers are encouraged to consider who they see in their neighborhoods.

LESSON VOCABULARY

live	out
people	who
work	

INTRODUCE THE BOOK

INTRODUCE THE TITLE AND AUTHOR Point to the book title, and challenge students to read this word. Confirm that the title is *Look at My Neighborhood*, then read the author's and illustrator's names, too. Let children describe or identify the type of neighborhood they see on the cover.

BUILD BACKGROUND Ask children if they think all neighborhoods are the same, and have children share what neighborhoods have in common. Lead children to the concept that neighborhoods are places where people live. Then have children describe features that might make neighborhoods different, such as buildings, parks, streets, and physical features. Mention that all neighborhoods have features that make them special and unique.

PREVIEW/TAKE A PICTURE WALK Invite children to leaf through the book to become familiar with its format. Ask children if the story is told by one child or by many children. Point out and discuss the beginning text on each page.

ELL Ahead of time, collect pictures of a group of people, homes, and people working. Use the pictures to reinforce vocabulary. Help children say simple sentences using the vocabulary words. For example: I see many people. I see homes where people live. People come out of their homes to go to work.

READ THE BOOK

SET PURPOSE Remind children that as they read, they should pause and ask questions about the text to help clarify what they read. Suggest that children pause after each page, and then think of a question to ask about it. Tell children to reread the text or study the illustrations to find the answers.

STRATEGY SUPPORT: IMPORTANT IDEAS Remind children that stories can have many ideas. Some ideas are more important than others. Good readers look for important ideas as they read. Important ideas tell readers more about the main idea. Ask children what important ideas they think they will find in *Look at My Neighborhood*.

COMPREHENSION QUESTIONS

PAGE 1 What type of neighborhood is this? *(a city)*

PAGE 4 What question can you ask about this neighborhood? *(What place is this? How do I know it is a farm?)*

PAGE 6 What job is shown here? How do you know? *(He is a police officer. He is wearing a uniform with a badge.)*

PAGE 8 Why does the author end this book with a question? *(The author wants children to think about their own neighborhoods.)*

REVISIT THE BOOK

THINK AND SHARE

1. Possible response: The author wants us to know about many neighborhoods.
2. Possible responses: I learned that there are many kinds of neighborhoods. This helped me see that people like different places for different reasons.
3. *pitch, catch*
4. Possible responses: The streets are not very crowded. The buildings are not very tall. I see a bakery, so this might be the main street of a town.

EXTEND UNDERSTANDING Have children look at the story characters on page 8 and notice details about them. Challenge children to recall the neighborhood in which each character lived. For example, one girl has a baseball bat. Where did she live? Two children wear bike helmets. Where did they live? Have children find the characters in the book and describe that neighborhood.

RESPONSE OPTIONS

WRITING Describe a postcard to children: a picture on one side, and a place to write a letter and address on the other side. Pass out large index cards. Have children draw pictures of their neighborhoods on the blank side. On the lined side, ask them to write sentences about their neighborhoods. Have them write classmates' names on the cards and "send" the postcards for others to read.

SPEAKING Have children imagine that the characters in the book visit their neighborhoods. Ask: What would you like to show them? Invite children to pretend they are giving a neighborhood tour, using sentences that describe their neighborhoods.

SOCIAL STUDIES CONNECTION

Time For SOCIAL STUDIES

Have children consider which neighborhood in the book is most like their own. Encourage children to exchange ideas about how the neighborhoods are similar and different.

Skill Work

TEACH/REVIEW VOCABULARY

Write sentences on the board for each of the vocabulary words. Omit the vocabulary words, and read the sentences. Write the missing words on cards, and have children place each word in the correct sentence.

TARGET SKILL AND STRATEGY

AUTHOR'S PURPOSE Mention to children that the *author's purpose* is the reason why an author chose to write a story. Speculate why an author might choose to write about a variety of neighborhoods. For example, the author may want readers to learn about the different places where people live.

IMPORTANT IDEAS Tell children that *important ideas* tell more about the main idea of a story. Ask: What are some important ideas in *Look at My Neighborhood*? How do you know these are important? *(Possible responses: Many people live and work in a city. There are many animals in the country. People play catch in the city. People ride bikes in a town. People swim in a lake.; All these ideas tell more about the main idea, how neighborhoods can be different.)*

ADDITIONAL SKILL INSTRUCTION

COMPARE/CONTRAST Share with children that when they compare two things, they notice how they are similar and different; when they contrast two things, they see how only two things are different. Help children compare and contrast the different neighborhoods they discover in this book. Draw a Venn diagram on the board and choose two neighborhoods to compare. As they notice similarities, record their ideas in the center portion of the diagram. As they notice differences, write their ideas in the outer circles of the diagram.

Name _____

Author's Purpose

Look at the picture and **read** the words.

Come and see my neighborhood.
We can walk in the park.

Why do you think the author wrote about a park in a city?

_____
- -
_____
- -
_____
- -
_____
- -
_____
- -
_____

Name _____

Vocabulary

Complete each sentence with a word from the box.

Words to Know
live   out   people   who   work

1. Neighborhoods are full of _____ .

2. Let's go _____ to meet them!

3. Sam and Pam _____ at the pet store.

4. This is Hal and Val. They _____ here.

5. What is your neighborhood like? _____ will
   we meet in your neighborhood?

The Dinosaur Herds

SUMMARY This book provides information about dinosaurs that lived in groups, or herds.

LESSON VOCABULARY

down	inside
now	there
together	

INTRODUCE THE BOOK

INTRODUCE THE TITLE AND AUTHOR Discuss with children the title and author of *The Dinosaur Herds*. Review with children the meaning of *herd (a group of animals that live together)*. Ask them if they know of any animals that live in herds. Ask them how the title helps them know what the book will be about.

BUILD BACKGROUND Inform children that some dinosaurs lived in herds. Encourage children to relate what they know about other animals in herds to what they think they might learn about dinosaurs and herds. Additionally, invite children to share whatever knowledge they have about dinosaurs.

PREVIEW/TAKE A PICTURE WALK Invite children to look at the pictures in the book. Ask them if they know the names of any of the dinosaurs in the pictures. Discuss what they think they might learn from the book. Write down any questions they hope the book will answer and revisit the questions after reading.

ELL Go over what is happening in the illustrations. Use the vocabulary words as you discuss the pictures.

READ THE BOOK

SET PURPOSE Have children set a purpose for reading *The Dinosaur Herds*. Children's interest in dinosaurs should guide this purpose. Using age-appropriate language, suggest children consider how groups of dinosaurs might work together to ensure their survival.

STRATEGY SUPPORT: INFERRING Explain to children that *inferring* is taking what you already know and what's in the story to guess about something the author didn't mention. You can often infer things from pictures or illustrations. Encourage children to make inferences as they read the story.

COMPREHENSION QUESTIONS

PAGES 5–7 What are some good things about being in a herd? *(Possible responses: Animals work together to eat in safety, hunt, build nests, and keep eggs safe.)*

PAGE 6 What might be a reason that some dinosaurs hunted together? *(Together they could jump on an animal and push it down.)*

PAGE 7 What is one way to better understand what a dinosaur nest might look like? *(Possible response: look at the picture on page 7)*

PAGE 8 Where is a place you can find information about dinosaurs? *(inside a book)*

REVISIT THE BOOK

THINK AND SHARE

1. First: Dinosaurs could get around and on top of the animal. Next: The herd could push the animal down. Last: The dinosaurs could eat the animal.
2. Small dinosaurs stayed inside the herd's circle and larger dinosaurs kept predators away from them. This helped me understand that some herds protect one another.
3. don't
4. Possible response: The pictures show that dinosaurs did not all look the same, live in the same environment, or act the same.

EXTEND UNDERSTANDING Revisit what children hoped to learn from reading the book. What questions developed in previewing did the book answer? Were they answered by reading the text, looking at the pictures, or both? After reading, do children have new questions about dinosaurs and herds? Let them know they can use the library or classroom books to get more information.

RESPONSE OPTIONS

WRITING Invite children to write a short poem about dinosaurs working together in a herd using information from this book.

SCIENCE CONNECTION

Display a variety of books about dinosaurs. Invite children to look at the books and then share two things they learned with the rest of their groups.

Skill Work

TEACH/REVIEW VOCABULARY

Make sure that children can see a list of the vocabulary words. Going around in a circle, have each child use a vocabulary word in a sentence.

TARGET SKILL AND STRATEGY

SEQUENCE Tell children that a good way to understand information in a book is to be clear about the order in which events happen. Encourage children to pay attention to the order of events that take place when the herds take care of their young. Review the graphic organizer in the back of the book. Let children know that they will be making one and filling it in after reading.

INFERRING Remind children that *inferring* is making a guess about something in a story the author didn't mention. Have children read pages 4 and 5. Ask: Why does the herd protect the baby dinosaur? Who wants to hurt the baby dinosaur?

ADDITIONAL SKILL INSTRUCTION

DRAW CONCLUSIONS Explain that good readers use both the words and pictures in a book, as well as their own knowledge, to make decisions about what they are reading. As children read, have them consider: Did anything surprise them? If they have discussed other animal herds in the Build Background section, have them compare that information to what they have learned about dinosaurs. Ask: Can they make any decisions about dinosaur herds based on prior knowledge? Afterwards have children discuss these decisions.

Name _____

Sequence

Use the boxes below to make a picture story of how the dinosaur herds hunt. Make sure your pictures are in the order of what really happens.

1.	2.

3.

Name _____

Vocabulary

Words to Know
down   inside   now   there   together

Choose a vocabulary word that is the opposite of each of the following words. Write it in the space next to each word.

1. outside   _____

2. alone   _____

3. here   _____

4. up   _____

5. later   _____

People Help the Forest

SUMMARY Many plants and animals live in a forest, like squirrels, bears, and birds. Readers are encouraged to take care of the forest and the things that live there.

LESSON VOCABULARY

around	find	food
grow	under	water

INTRODUCE THE BOOK

INTRODUCE THE TITLE AND AUTHOR Invite children to read the book title and author's name on their own. Guide children as necessary. Speculate with children what they think the book title means. Ask: Why might a forest need help? Which people do you think help a forest? List children's ideas on the board to check after reading.

BUILD BACKGROUND Show children a picture of a clean, pristine forest, and ask them to describe it. Ask children what lives in a forest, and confirm that many animals and plants live there. Then ask children what people do when they visit a forest. Help children recognize that when people visit a forest, they can have an effect—sometimes good, sometimes bad—on the forest and the plants and animals that live there.

PREVIEW Invite children to look through the book to prepare for reading. Focus attention on the photographs on page 5, and ask children to describe what the people in the photographs are doing. Turn to pages 6 and 7, and ask children how these photographs of a forest differ from the photograph on page 3.

READ THE BOOK

SET PURPOSE Discuss with children why and how they might want to help a forest. Based on this discussion, have them set their own purpose for reading the selection. Invite volunteers to share their purpose with the class.

STRATEGY SUPPORT: BACKGROUND KNOWLEDGE Remind children to use what they already know to help them understand what they are reading. As they read, remind them of the information shared before reading and have them connect this information to the text.

COMPREHENSION QUESTIONS

PAGE 5 Why might people visit a forest in summer? *(The weather is warm.)*

PAGE 6 What happened to the animals' homes on this page? *(The animals' homes were destroyed.)*

PAGE 8 Why should it be the job of the people who visit a forest to help the forest? *(Possible response: The people who visit the forest sometimes hurt the forest. They need to fix the things they have hurt.)*

REVISIT THE BOOK

THINK AND SHARE

1. Possible response: The author wants readers to learn how people can affect a forest. Possible response for web: protect the animals' homes; make sure animals have food; keep the forest clean; keep the forest beautiful so we can visit it
2. Possible response: I knew that a forest is home to many animals. This helped me understand why forests need help.
3. the long *u* sound
4. They put out fires; they cut down sick trees; they plant new trees.

EXTEND UNDERSTANDING

Point out to children that each page has a main picture and a smaller picture. Prompt children to explain how the smaller picture relates to the main picture and the text. For example, one of the smaller pictures on page 3 shows a bird. Help children make the connection that birds are one of the creatures that live in forests (as mentioned in the text), like the forest in the bigger picture on page 3.

RESPONSE OPTIONS

WRITING Invite children to create small posters that tell others how to help the forest. Suggest that they copy this sentence: *Help the forest!* Then encourage them to complete this sentence: *Do not ___.* Tell children to illustrate their ideas too.

SCIENCE CONNECTION

Invite children to make flow charts that show something people use or do in a forest, how that action affects the forest, and how people can help. For example: *Fires destroy trees. Animals have fewer homes. People can plant more trees.*

Skill Work

TEACH/REVIEW VOCABULARY

Print each word on an index card. Have children read each card, one by one, then work with children to use each word in a sentence.

ELL Write each word on the board, saying it as you do. Use hand motions to explain the meaning of each word. Have children follow your motions as they repeat the words.

TARGET SKILL AND STRATEGY

AUTHOR'S PURPOSE Confirm that an *author's purpose* is the reason why an author chose to write something. Speculate with children why the author might have chosen to write this book. For example, perhaps this author wanted to help people appreciate forests.

BACKGROUND KNOWLEDGE Mention to children that they can use what they already know to help them understand what they read. Have children use a KWL chart for *People Help the Forest* to generate questions for which they will look for answers as they read.

ADDITIONAL SKILL INSTRUCTION

CAUSE AND EFFECT Write the words *cause* and *effect* on the board. Set up a tower of blocks on the floor. Roll a ball along the floor so that it knocks over the blocks. Invite children to describe what has happened. Identify their ideas as cause and effect:

1. The rolling ball is the cause. It caused something to happen.
2. The falling blocks are the effect. The effect of the rolling ball is that the blocks fell.

Have children turn to page 7. Point to the photograph, and explain that this picture shows an effect. Speculate with children what caused this effect, and confirm that it was a fire.

Cause: fire ⟶ Effect: plant new trees
Cause: new trees ⟶ Effect: more animal homes

Name _____

Author's Purpose

Look at the picture and read the sentences.

A lot of people came to this forest. They played in the water. They looked at the birds and animals and trees.

Now the forest could use help. Some people who came did not take care of the forest.

Why do you think the author wrote about this forest? Use the words in the box to fill in the blanks.

> look   help   forest   safe

1. The author cares about the _____ .

2. The author wants others to _____ the forest.

3. The author likes to _____ at birds.

4. The author wants animals to be _____ .

Name _____

Vocabulary

Complete this puzzle. Write the word in the crossword puzzle that matches the definition. Write the words down, not across.

> ## Words to Know
>
> around   find   food   grow   under   water

1. a liquid
2. to get bigger
3. something to eat
4. when you look for something and get it
5. beneath or below

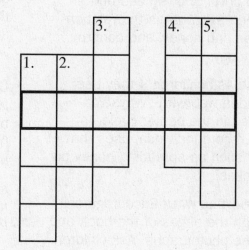

After you have filled in the puzzle, find the mystery word. It is missing one letter. Fill in the letter and complete the word.

_____

- -

_____

Honey

SUMMARY One of the jobs that bees do is make honey. People use honey in many ways, including adding it to food and drinks and putting it in bath water.

LESSON VOCABULARY

also	family
new	other
some	their

INTRODUCE THE BOOK

INTRODUCE THE TITLE AND AUTHOR Read aloud the book title and author's name with children. Point out that the cover shows bees and a bowl of honey. Then ask what is the relationship between bees and honey, and confirm that bees make honey.

BUILD BACKGROUND Ask children if they use honey. Begin an idea web with "Ways We Use Honey" printed in the center circle. In the outer circles, record individual uses that children suggest, such as spreading honey on toast or on pancakes.

PREVIEW/TAKE A PICTURE WALK Encourage children to flip through the pages of the book and to comment on the photographs. Ask children to identify the two images on page 4, and talk about how honey and a picnic basket might be connected. Also have children describe what they see on pages 6 and 7, and discuss how these images might relate to honey.

READ THE BOOK

SET PURPOSE Help children set a purpose for reading this book. Encourage them to think about what they would like to learn. For example, perhaps they would like to learn if the ways they use honey are mentioned in the book. Direct children to look for their ideas as they read.

STRATEGY SUPPORT: QUESTIONING Explain to children that good readers ask questions while they read. This helps them make sure that they understand what they are reading. Model asking a question on page 3: The story says that some bees have many jobs. What jobs do they have? Encourage children to come up with their own questions as they read.

COMPREHENSION QUESTIONS

PAGE 3 Compare and contrast the connection between bees and honey, and people and honey. *(Bees make and use honey. People only use honey, they do not make it.)*

PAGE 5 Why would someone use honey to make bread? *(Possible response: They want the bread to taste sweeter.)*

PAGE 6 How can honey help when you are sick? *(Possible response: It may help us feel good.)*

REVISIT THE BOOK

THINK AND SHARE

1. Possible responses: Honey and sugar both make things sweet. Honey and sugar are different colors and they come from different things.

2. Possible response: What ways do we use honey? It helped me identify the many uses for honey as I read.

3. *c, v, c, c, v, c*; responses will vary.

4. Possible responses: Honey is a liquid. Honey is thick. Honey is a golden color. Honey can be poured.

EXTEND UNDERSTANDING Work with children to make a chain of events that connects people to bees. Start with bees on the left side of the "chain" and people on the far right side. Then have children fill in the blanks to explain how bees and people are connected. For example: Bees build hives. Bees visit flowers. Bees collect nectar. Bees make honey in their hives. People remove the honey. People enjoy the honey.

RESPONSE OPTIONS

WRITING Have children write thank-you cards to the bees, thanking them for making honey. On the outside of their cards, have children write, "Thank you, bees!" Tell children to illustrate the outside too. Ask children to mention the ways that people use honey on the inside of their cards.

WORD WORK Have children create sentences that tell others why they should try honey. Encourage them to use the vocabulary words in their sentences and to mimic their sentences after commercials, for example, "Use honey! Your family will love this sweet treat!"

SCIENCE CONNECTION

Invite children to think of other animals and plants we depend on. List the animals and plants and the food or other products we get from them, for example: cows—milk; chickens—eggs; cotton—clothing; sheep—wool.

Skill Work

TEACH/REVIEW VOCABULARY

Write sentences that each use a vocabulary word. Say a vocabulary word and point to its sentence. Then read the sentence with the group. Encourage children to explain the meaning of the word in context.

ELL Show children a picture of a family with something new, such as a baby or car. Use vocabulary words to talk about the picture. Write each vocabulary word as you say it. Have children read the word and say it with you.

TARGET SKILL AND STRATEGY

COMPARE AND CONTRAST Share with children that when they say how two things are alike, they tell how they are the same. When they say how two things are different, they tell how they are not the same. Have children *compare and contrast* the pictures on pages 4 and 5 with the pictures on pages 6 and 7. Ask: How are the pictures alike? *(They show what honey is used for.)* How are the pictures different? *(We see honey on pages 4 and 5 but not on pages 6 or 7.)*

QUESTIONING Remind children that asking questions as you read can help you figure out what you don't understand. Have children create a T-Chart with the titles *Questions* and *Answers*. As they read, have them write any questions they have under the *Questions* column. Then have them write the answers in the *Answers* column.

ADDITIONAL SKILL INSTRUCTION

DRAW CONCLUSIONS Tell children they should use what they read, see, and know about real life to figure out more about what happens in the book. Model page 5: I read that honey is used when people bake bread and cakes. I know that people bake more than bread and cakes. I think that honey can be used in cookies and pies too. After page 4, ask: Why would you take honey on a picnic?

Name _____

Compare and Contrast

Read the paragraphs.

Some people eat honey when they are sick. Can honey help them feel better? Some people hope honey will make them feel better.

Some people put honey in the bath. They mix honey with the water. They use honey to make their skin soft.

1. What are both paragraphs about?

2. How are the paragraphs different?

58

Name _____

Vocabulary

Complete each sentence with a word from the box.

Words to Know
also   family   new   Other   Some   Their

_____
1. _____ people bake with it.

_____
2. _____ people bathe with it!

_____
3. You can _____ eat it, of course.

_____
4. How does your _____ use it?

_____
5. _____ ways may be different from yours.

_____
6. Try to think of a _____ way to use it.

7. Write a sentence of your own using one or two words
   from the box.

   _____

   _____

   _____

Let's Build a Park!

SUMMARY A group of friends has nothing to do and nowhere to play, so they decide to build a park in their neighborhood.

LESSON VOCABULARY

always	become
day	everything
nothing	stays
things	

INTRODUCE THE BOOK

INTRODUCE THE TITLE AND AUTHOR Discuss with children the title and the author of *Let's Build a Park!* Have children look at the cover and ask: What do you think the characters in this illustration are doing? Why do you think that?

BUILD BACKGROUND Discuss the neighborhood in which your school is located. Ask: Are there any parks in the neighborhood? What types of things do people like to do in a park? Have children speculate about how the parks got there.

PREVIEW Have children examine the cover of the book. Then have them turn the pages and look at the illustrations. Together, brainstorm a list of predictions about what the story might be about. Record children's ideas on the board or on chart paper for later review.

READ THE BOOK

SET PURPOSE Have children set a purpose for reading *Let's Build a Park*! Suggest that children think about why a new park is being built.

STRATEGY SUPPORT: SUMMARIZE Summarizing helps children recall and comprehend the main ideas in the text. Encourage children to ask what the main idea of the book is as they read. Remind children that a summary answers the questions *Who?* and *What happened?*

COMPREHENSION QUESTIONS

PAGE 3 Why did the children decide to build a park? *(because they had nothing to do and no place to play)*

PAGE 4 What did the children do first? *(planted trees)*

PAGE 5 Who helped build swings? *(Mom)*

PAGES 6 What kind of seeds do you think were planted in the garden to make the park pretty? *(flower seeds)*

REVISIT THE BOOK

THINK AND SHARE

1. planted trees; built swings; planted a garden.
2. This story is about friends who build a park. Their families help build the park too. They put trees, a garden, and swings in their park.
3. Possible response: I *always* brush my teeth in the morning.
4. Possible response: They could play baseball. They could have a picnic.

EXTEND UNDERSTANDING After children have read the story, discuss what happened *first*, *next*, and *last*. Point out that the text and the illustrations help us to determine the order in which events occur.

RESPONSE OPTIONS

WRITING Suggest that children write a few sentences describing what they would put in a park that they built. Have them draw a picture of their park.

DRAMA CONNECTION Assign roles to children and have them act out scenes from *Let's Build a Park!*

Skill Work

TEACH/REVIEW VOCABULARY

Print each vocabulary word on an index card. Show the cards one at a time. Ask: What is the first letter in this word? Does this word have a smaller word inside it? Read the words aloud as a group. Then display them on the word wall.

ELL Distribute vocabulary word cards and have children go on a scavenger hunt to look for the same word in other classroom books or written materials.

TARGET SKILL AND STRATEGY

SEQUENCE Remind children that *sequence* is the order in which things happen. Suggest that children consider the order of events described in this book. For example, ask: What happened after the boy and his friends decided the neighborhood needed a park? *(His parents helped plant trees and build swings.)* What happened next? *(They planted seeds for a garden.)*

SUMMARIZE Point out that a summary of a story is a short description of the characters and the main ideas in the story. Remind children that understanding the plot of the story makes it easier to do a summary. As children read, have them look for the main characters and the most important story events.

ADDITIONAL SKILL INSTRUCTION

AUTHOR'S PURPOSE Remind children that authors always have a reason for writing. Point out that *Let's Build a Park!* is not only entertaining, but it gives good information about a neighborhood building a park. Suggest that children think about other reasons the author might have written this book. Explain that knowing the author's purpose will help them better understand what they read.

Name _____

Sequence

Below are sentences based on the story. They are not in the correct order. Number the sentences from 1−5 so that they are in the order in which they happened in *Let's Build a Park!*

_____ **a.** Mom helped us build swings.

_____ **b.** An empty lot has become a park!

_____ **c.** We got some seeds.

_____ **d.** Someone said, "Let's build a park!"

_____ **e.** Dad planted trees.

What kinds of things can the people in the story do in their new park? Write your answers on the lines below.

_____

_____

_____

_____

Name _____

Vocabulary

Pick a word from the box to finish each sentence.
Write it on the line.

Words to Know

always   become   day   everything
nothing   stays   things

1. My mom can do lots of _____.

2. My dad _____ helps me when I need it.

3. My friend _____ at the park a long time.

4. When we go to the park, we want to do _____.

5. Each _____ we do something new.

6. When I grow up, maybe I will _____ a builder.

7. _____ is as much fun as a trip to the park.

Mac Can Do It!

SUMMARY In this fantasy, newborn infant Mac learns at a super-human rate and amazes his parents. A time line at the end of the book summarizes Mac's incredible accomplishments.

LESSON VOCABULARY

any	enough
ever	every
own	sure
were	

INTRODUCE THE BOOK

INTRODUCE THE TITLE AND AUTHOR Discuss with children the title and the author of *Mac Can Do It!* Based on the title and the cover illustration, ask children what they think might happen in this story.

BUILD BACKGROUND Discuss what children know about babies and their development. If they have experience with newborn babies, have them talk about what babies can and cannot do.

PREVIEW Ask children to turn the pages of the book and look at the illustrations to predict what will happen in this story.

READ THE BOOK

SET PURPOSE Have children set a purpose for reading *Mac Can Do It!* This purpose should relate to the structure or content of the story. Children might choose to look for important story events or examples of fantasy.

STRATEGY SUPPORT: INFERRING Encourage children to use what they know to make a guess, or an inference, about Mac. Help them think about Mac based on the information in the story. Ask children what they can infer about Mac and why they made their conclusion. Have them use the illustrations and text in the book to help explain their reasoning.

COMPREHENSION QUESTIONS

PAGE 5 Do you think a two-week old baby is old enough to run in a race? Is this part of the story real or make-believe? *(Two-week old babies cannot walk or run; this is make-believe.)*

PAGE 7 How did Mac's mom feel when he fixed the sink for her? How can you tell? *(She was surprised and happy. The illustrations show that she is smiling.)*

PAGE 11 What does it mean when the book says, "Mac was not just any boy"? *(Mac does things that other babies cannot do.)*

PAGES 10-11 What do you think happens after Mac takes off in his spaceship? *(Responses will vary.)*

REVISIT THE BOOK

THINK AND SHARE

1. Possible response: Mac can read numbers at four weeks old. I read numbers at 4 years old. We are alike because we can both read numbers. We are different because Mac read numbers much sooner than I did.
2. Possible response: We know he can read numbers because he is writing numbers on a chalkboard. Responses about understanding will vary.
3. *mailman, mailbox; mail*
4. Responses will vary but should include personal episodes from the reader's life.

EXTEND UNDERSTANDING As children read the book, ask them to think about how the illustrations support the story. What do they learn about the characters by looking at the illustrations?

RESPONSE OPTIONS

WORD WORK Make a word-and-picture card for the compound word *mailman*. Draw mail and a man on one side and print the word *mailman* on the other side. Show the picture to the children and have them guess the word. Then invite them to make word-and-picture cards for other compound words.

SOCIAL STUDIES CONNECTION

Have children bring in baby photos of themselves for a class display. Encourage them to discuss what they did as babies and how they have learned and grown since then.

Skill Work

TEACH/REVIEW VOCABULARY

Divide children into pairs. Give each pair a list of vocabulary words, a highlighter, and an old newspaper or magazine. Have the children highlight the vocabulary words they find.

ELL Print vocabulary words on pairs of blank index cards. Invite children to play a concentration game. As they turn over the cards, have the children read the words aloud.

TARGET SKILL AND STRATEGY

COMPARE AND CONTRAST Remind children that when they compare two things, they tell how they are the same. When they contrast two things, they tell how they are different. After reading pages 4 and 5, have children compare and contrast Mac with the other children in the race.

INFERRING Point out that making an inference means making a guess based on information from the book. Remind children that they should use what they read and then form an idea or make a guess based on that information. Have children make an inference about Mac's mom and dad. What information did they use to make their guess?

ADDITIONAL SKILL INSTRUCTION

REALISM AND FANTASY Discuss the difference between realism and fantasy. A *realistic* story tells about something that could happen in real life. A *fantasy* is make-believe. Read page 3 together and ask children if they think that it is realistic for a one-week old baby to talk. Why not? Encourage children to look for other examples of fantasy as they read.

Name _____

Compare and Contrast

Think about Mac and his mom and dad. In the diagram below, write about Mac and his mom and dad. In the middle, write how they are both alike.

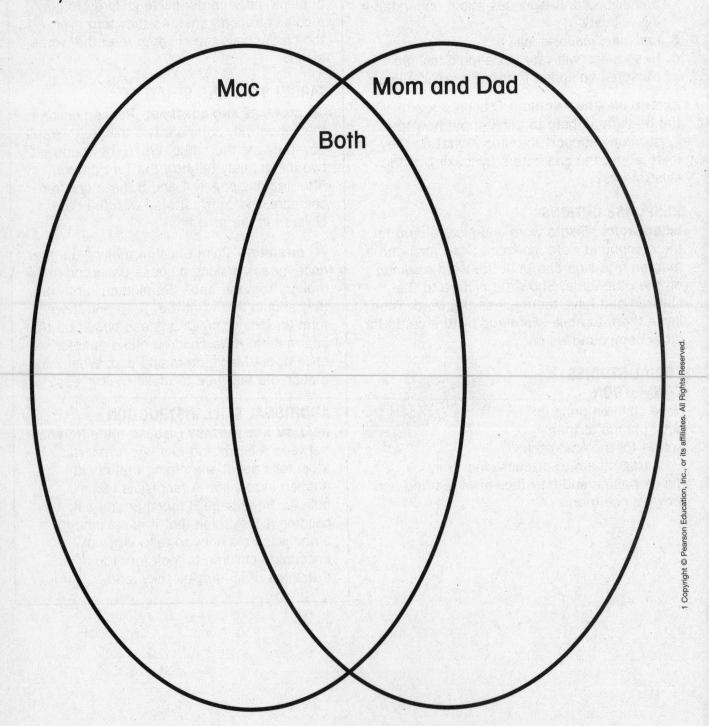

Mac

Mom and Dad

Both

Name _____

Vocabulary

Find these words in the puzzle. Circle them.
Words may be across or down.

Words to Know

any	enough	ever	every
own	sure	were	

```
e  v  e  r     r     a  g
y  w  r  e     e     y  y
s  e  y  e     n     r  n
u  o  y  w  w     e  r
r  w  e  r  e     e  a
e  n  o  u  g     h  n
e  v  e  r     y  w  y
```

Big Wishes and Her Baby

SUMMARY Lori tells about Mom's riding school near their house. Big Wishes is Mom's horse. Big Wishes just had a baby girl horse. Big Wishes is a good mom. Lori is a good helper at Mom's riding school. She helps Mom with chores around the school.

LESSON VOCABULARY

away	car	friends
house	our	school
very		

INTRODUCE THE BOOK

INTRODUCE THE TITLE AND AUTHOR Before reading the book title, ask children what they think the people on the cover of the book are doing. Elicit ideas; then read the title, as well as the author and illustrator's names, to the group. Speculate with children why people might be brushing horses, and then talk about where people would do this. Encourage children to explain why people enjoy taking care of horses.

BUILD BACKGROUND Have children describe or identify places where they have seen horses. List their ideas on the board. Then ask children what the horses were doing. For example, were they carrying people? Were they wearing a saddle? Explain to children that horses are used in many ways.

PREVIEW Prompt children to look through the book, explore the illustrations, and become familiar with the placement of text. As children study pages 8 and 9, ask them to describe how the people take care of the horses. Ask children what else people might do to take care of horses.

READ THE BOOK

SET PURPOSE Help children form a purpose for reading. Ask children what they would like to discover as they read this book. For example, perhaps children want to know where horses live. Write the purpose on the board, encouraging children to look for this purpose as they read.

STRATEGY SUPPORT: MONITOR AND CLARIFY Mention to children that sometimes when they read, they form an idea about the text. When they reread the text, however, they may discover that they misunderstood what they read. Demonstrate monitoring and clarifying for the group. For example, read the text on page 6, then question yourself: "Hmm. Is the baby horse ready for visitors today?" Then, reread the text, and clarify your ideas. "Yes today is the first day the baby horse can have visitors. She is now old enough."

COMPREHENSION QUESTIONS

PAGE 4 What does Lori's mom do? (*Possible responses: She teaches kids about riding. She owns a riding school.*)

PAGE 7 Is Big Wishes a good mom? How do you know? (*Yes. She watches her baby play with the children.*)

PAGE 8 How often do the horses need to be taken care of? (*everyday*) Why do the horses need hay and grain? (*Possible response: They eat hay and grain.*)

PAGE 10 Why does the baby horse need special food? (*Possible response: The baby horse's special food helps it grow. The baby horse might not be ready for regular horse food.*)

REVIVIT THE BOOK

THINK AND SHARE

1. Facts: Food helps baby horses grow. Horses need to be taken care of everyday. Opinions: Horses loved to be brushed. The baby loves to play tag.
2. Responses will vary.
3. Responses will vary but should be based on places near and far from children's houses.
4. Possible response: I would enjoy being around the horses. One of my jobs would be brushing the horses.

EXTEND UNDERSTANDING Read with children the text on page 8. Have children apply what they learn in the text to the riding school in the story. Help children make the connection and arrive at the theme, or "big idea," that horses, even mother horses, need to be taken care of everyday. Ask children to name some of the ways that the horses in the story were taken care of. Encourage children to consider other ways in which horses are taken care of.

RESPONSE OPTIONS

WRITING Have children imagine that the people at the riding school want to invite the community for an open house to meet the baby horse. What might the invitation say? Ask children to write an invitation inviting everyone to the riding school.

SPEAKING AND LISTENING Remind children that running a riding school is a lot of work. Suggest that Lori's mom won an award for excellence in teaching children to ride horses. What might the award presenter say to Lori's mom? What might Lori's mom say in return? Encourage children to give speeches in the role of the award presenter or Lori's mom.

SOCIAL STUDIES CONNECTION

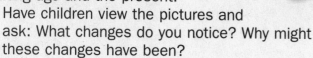

Try to find pictures of farms and ranches from long ago and the present. Have children view the pictures and ask: What changes do you notice? Why might these changes have been?

Skill Work

TEACH/REVIEW VOCABULARY

Write a simple sentence strip for each vocabulary word. Display a strip, say the vocabulary word, and have children scan for the word. Ask a volunteer to point to it. Then read the sentence, and discuss the word's meaning within the context of that sentence. Continue with the next word.

ELL Show children four pictures: a *house*, a *car*, a *school*, and a group of *friends*. After you say one of these four vocabulary words, ask children to point to the picture that shows what the word means. Have children say each word with you.

TARGET SKILL AND STRATEGY

FACT AND OPINION Help children understand the difference between facts and opinions. Facts are ideas you can prove. Opinions are ideas that people think but cannot prove. Ask children to look at page 9. The sentence *We also brush each horse* is a fact. The picture on the page can prove it. Have children look at page 7. The sentence *The baby loves to play tag* is an opinion. We cannot prove that the baby loves to play tag. It is only someone's belief that the baby loves to play tag.

MONITOR AND CLARIFY Instruct children to pause after they read each page to consider what has happened so far in the story. To make sure they have understood everything correctly, tell children to reread the page and to revise, or clarify, any misconceptions. Remind children that correcting their understanding can help them understand the big idea of the story.

ADDITIONAL SKILL INSTRUCTION

CAUSE AND EFFECT Explain to children that an effect is what happens, and a cause is why it happens. Give children some examples, such as Cause: You spend the whole day playing in the hot sun; Effect: You get a sunburn. Cause: There is a very bad snow storm; Effect: There is a "snow day" and school is canceled. Ask children to suggest a cause and effect from the book.

Name _____

Fact and Opinion

A **fact** is a piece of information that can be proven to be true. An **opinion** is a piece of information that someone thinks, but cannot be proven.

1. Read the sentences. Circle the opinions that are from *Big Wishes and Her Baby*.

   a. Big Wishes is my mom's horse.

   b. Big Wishes is a very good mom.

   c. We brush each horse.

   d. Horses love to be brushed.

2-3. Write two facts from the story.

_____
- -
_____
_____
- -
_____
_____
- -
_____

Vocabulary

Complete the poster with words from the box.
Think about what makes the most sense.

> ## Words to Know
>
> away   car   friends   house
> our   school   very

Come One! Come All!
Come to Meet Big Wishes Baby

_____

_____

We are _____ proud to tell you that

_____

_____

_____ horse Big Wishes has a new baby!

_____

_____

Drive your _____ to visit the new baby horse.

_____

_____

Our riding _____ , is large, so everyone
can come.

_____   _____

_____   _____

Our _____ is not far _____ , so
join us for snacks too!

_____

_____

Bring your _____ !

We'll see you at the Riding School!

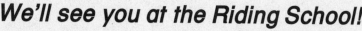

Plans Change

SUMMARY Mark's family plans a picnic with Nana. Their plans are spoiled, however, by the weather, or so they think. Mark is surprised to find that Nana has another idea. Mark learns that you can have fun whether it rains or not.

LESSON VOCABULARY

afraid	again
few	how
read	soon

INTRODUCE THE BOOK

INTRODUCE THE TITLE AND AUTHOR Discuss with students the title and the author of *Plans Change*. Talk about what it means to "change your plans." Ask: By reading the title and looking at the picture on the cover, what plans do you think this family had to change? Does the picture remind you of anything that your family has done?

BUILD BACKGROUND Invite children to talk about a time when their family had to change their plans because the weather wasn't what they expected it to be. Ask: What was planned at first? What kind of weather made you change your plans? What did you do instead? Have children share how they felt before, during, and after the change of plans.

PREVIEW Have children preview the book by looking at the pictures. Point out the expressions on the family's faces on each page. As they read, ask them to think about what happens first, next, and last.

READ THE BOOK

SET PURPOSE Set a purpose for reading *A Plans Change*. This should relate to questions from their preview. Suggest that children think about what plans the family had to change, and why the plans changed.

STRATEGY SUPPORT: VISUALIZE As children read, have them pause occasionally to close their eyes and visualize the action. Ask them to think aloud and describe what they see in their minds. Encourage children to be as specific as possible in their descriptions.

COMPREHENSION QUESTIONS

PAGE 3 What happens first in the story? *(Mark's family is planning a picnic with Nana.)*

PAGE 4-5 What items will Mark's family bring to the picnic? *(sports equipment, a blanket, and food)*

PAGE 6 What does Mom find out when she reads the paper? *(that it is supposed to rain the next day)*

PAGE 11 Try to visualize Nana's picnic. What do you see? *(Responses should include specific types of food that Nana set out.)*

REVISIT THE BOOK

THINK AND SHARE

1. Possible response: The author writes about a change in plans to tell children that sometimes things don't go as planned.
2. Responses will vary, but should reflect that they have combined their own experiences with details from the text to create a mental image.
3. *Mark, park, started, car*
4. Responses will vary.

EXTEND UNDERSTANDING Ask children to recall their predictions about the book. Did the change of plans turn out to be what they expected? Discuss events that occurred at the beginning, middle, and end of the story.

RESPONSE OPTIONS

WORD WORK Ask children to plan an indoor picnic for the classroom. Have them make a list of foods they would like to eat at the picnic. Then have them draw a picture of each food item.

SCIENCE CONNECTION

Have children keep a log of the weather each day for a week. Provide books about weather, and help children research the types of weather events that are experienced in your area.

TIME FOR Science

Skill Work

TEACH/REVIEW VOCABULARY

Print vocabulary words on index cards and scatter the cards face up on the floor or on a table. Call out words and then ask a volunteer to pick up the corresponding word card and use the word in a sentence.

ELL Ask English language learners to sort the vocabulary word cards according to initial letter, final letter, or number of syllables.

TARGET SKILL AND STRATEGY

AUTHOR'S PURPOSE Remind children that an author's purpose is the reason an author chooses to write something. Speculate with children why the author might have chosen to write this book. For example, perhaps this author wanted to help people know that it's okay if plans change.

VISUALIZE Remind children that good readers form pictures in their heads when they read a story. *Visualizing* helps readers understand what they are reading. Model as children read *Plans Change*: When I close my eyes, I can see a family in their grandmother's home. The family is eating, laughing, and having a good time. I see a colorful blanket spread on the floor. I see a lot of good things to eat and drink on the blanket.

ADDITIONAL SKILL INSTRUCTION

SETTING Point out to children that when they read a story, they can think about where and when the story takes place. This is called the *setting*. Knowing the setting can help readers understand what happens and why. Ask: Does this story happen in a place that is like a place you know, or is it a make-believe place? Encourage children to refer to details in the text and illustrations as they discuss the story's setting.

Name _____

Author's Purpose

Read the sentences.

> Many boys and girls like to ride bikes. They wear helmets when they ride. Helmets help keep them safe.
>
> Sometimes children ride their bikes on trails. Sometimes they ride their bikes to school or to the store. It is important to watch for cars and trucks when riding a bike.

Why do you think the author wrote about bicycles?
Use the words in the box to fill in the blanks.

Words to Know
safety   bike   cars   helmet

1. The author wants children to wear a _____ when riding a bike.

2. The author cares about children's _____ .

3. The author wants children to be aware of _____ when riding bikes.

4. The author likes to ride a _____ .

Name _____

Vocabulary

Fill in the blank with the word that best fits each sentence.

Words to Know
afraid again few how read soon

1. _____ these steps and learn about gardens.

2. First you plant a _____ seeds.

3. _____ you will have a beautiful garden.

4. You can learn _____ to grow seeds.

5. If your garden doesn't grow, try _____ .

6. Don't be _____ to try your plan.

Let's Visit a Butterfly Greenhouse

SUMMARY This nonfiction text depicts what people can see and learn at a butterfly greenhouse. The book also describes the exciting changes that take place at each stage of the butterfly life cycle.

LESSON VOCABULARY

done	know
push	visit
wait	

INTRODUCE THE BOOK

INTRODUCE THE TITLE AND AUTHOR Discuss with children the title and author of *Let's Visit a Butterfly Greenhouse*. Based on the title and cover photograph, ask the children what they might learn from this book. Also call attention to the *Science* label in the upper-left corner and ask children how they think the information in this book might be related to science.

BUILD BACKGROUND Engage children in a discussion about butterflies. Invite them to describe butterflies they have seen (size, shape, color). Ask: Where have you seen a butterfly? What else do you know about butterflies?

PREVIEW/TAKE A PICTURE WALK Have the children preview the book, looking at the pictures. Guide them in using the labels to understand and describe what they see in the photographs. Encourage them to use this information to make predictions about the text and what they might learn about in this book.

READ THE BOOK

SET PURPOSE Based on your discussion of the title and cover photographs, invite children to share what they would most like to learn about butterflies and butterfly greenhouses.

STRATEGY SUPPORT: TEXT STRUCTURE As children read, remind them that text is organized in a sequence to help us understand the information. Draw a set of four sequence frames on the board and have children assist you in drawing the stages in the butterfly life cycle as explained on pages 6–10.

COMPREHENSION QUESTIONS

PAGE 3 Why is it interesting to learn about an indoor home for butterlies? *(Possible response: because butterflies usually only live outdoors)*

PAGE 5 Why does a butterfly greenhouse have flowers? *(Butterflies drink flower nectar.)*

PAGES 7-9 Describe what a caterpillar does. What does this tell you about a caterpillar? *(Possible responses: pushes out of an egg, eats eggshells and plants, crawls and eats, and makes chrysalis. Caterpillar is busy; does many things.)*

PAGE 11 What do you think would be most interesting or exciting about visiting a butterfly greenhouse and why? *(Responses will vary; encourage children to use information they learned from the text to support and explain their answers.)*

REVISIT THE BOOK

THINK AND SHARE

1. Two opinions: Did you know that a butterfly greenhouse is an exciting place?, Did you know that people learn a lot at a butterfly greenhouse?. They are both opinions because it cannot be proven that a butterfly greenhouse is exciting or that people learn a lot at a butterfly greenhouse.
2. egg: page 6; butterfly: page 11
3. it's/it is
4. Possible responses: descriptions of size, color, and shape of chrysalis.

EXTEND UNDERSTANDING Invite the children to look again at the photographs in the book. Call attention to the labels and discuss how these can aid in comprehension and understanding. Ask: Why do you think the author included these labels with the photographs? How do the labels help us better understand the photographs and the text?

RESPONSE OPTIONS

WRITING Ask children to write a few sentences about what they might see at a butterfly greenhouse. Guide them in using signal words to organize and sequence their narrative (first, next, then, last).

SCIENCE CONNECTION

Provide additional books or magazines with information about butterflies. Children can create and illustrate their own diagrams of the butterfly life cycle.

Skill Work

TEACH/REVIEW VOCABULARY

Create a set of cards with a vocabulary word on each and give each card to a child. Make a set of sentence strips with the following sentences: *I am finished. I learned something. I moved the door. I went to see my friend. I stayed until the end.* Show each sentence and read it aloud. Ask children to show the vocabulary word that goes best with each sentence.

TARGET SKILL AND STRATEGY

FACT AND OPINION Help children understand the difference between a fact and an opinion. Facts are ideas that can be proven to be true. Opinions are ideas that people think or believe but cannot be proven. Have children find a fact in the book. How do they know it's a fact? Then have children find an opinion in the book. How do they know it's an opinion?

TEXT STRUCTURE As children read the book, help them identify and keep track of the stages of the butterfly life cycle. Model for the children how to use a graphic organizer to record the stages of the life cycle as they read. Use signal words (first, next, then, last) to organize the information.

ADDITIONAL SKILL INSTRUCTION

AUTHOR'S PURPOSE Remind the children that this is a nonfiction book and invite them to discuss why they think the author chose to write about this topic. Ask: Why do you think the author included information on the butterfly life cycle in this book?

ELL To reinforce signal word meanings, English language learners may also wish to write the words *first, next, then,* and *last* in their home languages alongside the English words.

Name _____

Fact and Opinion

Read each fact below. Than write an opinion about each fact.

1. Most caterpillars eat their egg shells. Many caterpillars also eat plants.

   Opinion:
   _____
   -
   _____
   -
   _____
   -
   _____

2. People can learn a lot at a butterfly greenhouse. You can watch a butterfly come out of its chrysalis there.

   Opinion:
   _____
   -
   _____
   -
   _____
   -
   _____

Name _____

Vocabulary

Find each of the following vocabulary words in *Let's Visit a Butterfly Greenhouse.* Write the page number on which you found the word.

Then write your own sentence using a vocabulary word.

1. done: page _____

2. know: page _____

3. push: page _____

4. visit: page _____

5. wait: page _____

_____

6. _____

Seasons Come and Go

SUMMARY People do different things to adjust to the weather in each season. So do plants and animals. This nonfiction text helps readers discover the seasonal changes of plants and animals. For example, bears hibernate in winter. The arctic fox's fur changes from white in winter to brown in summer. Flowers and leaves grow and die as the seasons change.

LESSON VOCABULARY

before	does
good-bye	oh
right	won't

INTRODUCE THE BOOK

INTRODUCE THE TITLE AND AUTHOR Point to the text on the cover, and make sure children know which is the *title* and which are the author and the illustrator's names. Then read them with the group. Have children compare the title with the cover illustration, and have them make observations. Confirm that the title does not reflect the images on the cover because the title mentions a flower and an animal, while the picture shows people. Ask children what the title and the picture do have in common, and confirm that one picture shows winter, while the other picture shows spring. Tell children to finger-trace a line from the words *winter* and *spring* to their corresponding pictures. Then predict with children what this book might be about.

BUILD BACKGROUND Invite children to consider how they dress differently for each season. If your area does not have dramatic seasonal changes, you might have children speculate what clothing people might wear in cooler weather. For example, what do people wear in the winter? in the spring and fall? Conclude that people make changes according to the seasons. Explain that plants and animals also make changes with the seasons.

PREVIEW/TAKE A PICTURE WALK Prompt children to look through the book. Have children pause on pages 6 and 7, and tell them to point to the text below each picture. Ask children what this text is, and confirm that this text is a label. Review with children that labels tell information about photographs or illustrations. Read these labels to preview the text. Encourage children to find additional labels in the book. (pages 8 and 9)

ELL Write each word on an index card. Hold up the card and say it for the group. Encourage children to say it with you. Make up sentences for each word and have children repeat each sentence.

READ THE BOOK

SET PURPOSE Suggest that children set a purpose for reading to help focus their attention. For example, perhaps children would like to know more about seasons. Tell them to look for information about the seasons as they read.

STRATEGY SUPPORT: BACKGROUND KNOWLEDGE Remind children that background knowledge is the information they already know about a topic. As they read, encourage children to consider what they know about how plants and animals change with the seasons. Have them compare what they know with the new information they learn.

COMPREHENSION QUESTIONS

PAGE 3 Which season is cold so that people need to wear warm clothing? *(winter)*

PAGE 5 Which season will come after winter? *(spring)*

PAGE 6 Why is it important for the fox to blend in with the snow and the ground? *(Blending in helps the fox to hide from animals who might want to catch it.)*

REVIST THE BOOK

THINK AND SHARE

1. In the spring it is sunny. The flowers and grass grow in the spring. In the fall it is cool. The leaves change color and the apples grow in the fall.
2. Possible response: I know that bears sleep all winter and wake up in the spring, and that some trees have no leaves in the winter. This helped me understand the pictures on pages 4–5 and 10–11.
3. Possible responses: *edges, hedge*
4. winter and summer

EXTEND UNDERSTANDING Speculate with children how plants and animals know that the seasons are changing. Elicit from children ways in which the weather and the days change throughout the year, encouraging them to draw on prior knowledge and experiences. For example, days become longer in summer and shorter in winter. The air becomes warmer in summer and cooler in winter. Ask children if they think plants and animals are aware of these changes. Have children explain their ideas.

RESPONSE OPTIONS

WRITING Speculate with children why this book is titled *Seasons Come and Go*. Have children write a sentence for each part of the title that explains how it relates to the changing season. Let children draw pictures for their sentences too.

WORD WORK Write the word *seasons* in the middle of a word web. In four surrounding circles, write each of the four seasons. Invite children to suggest words that describe each season. Write their words in the appropriate circles.

SCIENCE CONNECTION

Help children conduct research to learn about other plants or animals that change with the seasons.
For example, where do frogs go in winter? Where do bees go? How does corn grow throughout the year? Let children draw what they discover about how plants and animals change, in sequence.

Skill Work

TEACH/REVIEW VOCABULARY

Write the words on the board, then write and say words that mean the opposite. Have children match the words to show they know the meanings. For example: *good-bye/hello*; *right/wrong*; *before/after*.

TARGET SKILL AND STRATEGY

DRAW CONCLUSIONS Call children's attention to pages 8¬–9 and model for them how to draw conclusions about the text. Say: Here I read that in the winter the hedge has no roses. Later in the spring the roses grow on the hedge. This information tells me that there are some changes that take place between the winter and the spring.

BACKGROUND KNOWLEDGE Share with children that *prior knowledge* refers to things they know before they begin reading. This knowledge helps them to better understand what they read. Invite children to share what they already know about how plants or animals change with the seasons. Then discuss the order of these changes.

ADDITIONAL SKILL INSTRUCTION

COMPARE AND CONTRAST Review with children that when they look at two things, they can notice how the two things are alike and how they are different. Explain that thinking about likenesses and differences helps them broaden their understanding. Work with children to make comparisons in the text.

1. On either side of a T-chart write *Bear in Fall* and *Bear in Spring*.

2. Have children study the picture of the bear on page 4. As children describe the bear and the scenery, write their ideas on the T-chart: *The bear is round and big. The leaves are falling*.

3. Then ask children to describe the bear and the scenery on page 5, and record those ideas as well.

Name _____

Draw Conclusions

Read each set of information.
Then draw a conclusion and write it on the lines.

1. In the winter, a fox's coat gets white. It looks just like snow.

    Conclusion:

    _____
    _____
    _____
    _____
    _____
    _____
    _____
    _____
    _____

2. In the summer, a fox's fur gets brown. It looks just like the ground.

    Conclusion:

    _____
    _____
    _____
    _____
    _____
    _____
    _____

Name _____

Vocabulary

Write the word from the box that best fits in each sentence.

Words to Know		
before	does	good-bye
oh	right	won't

_____

1. _____ the winter comes, a bear must eat and eat.

_____

2. The bear _____ this to become fat.

_____

3. If it doesn't eat, the bear _____ sleep.

_____

4. The bear waits until the time is _____ .

_____

5. Then it is time to say _____ until spring.

_____

6. _____ , hello, bear! It is spring again!

Special Days, Special Food

SUMMARY Children can read about how special celebrations call for special food, and they can see that it happens all over the world. Party foods in China, France, Mexico, Cuba, and an American backyard are highlighted.

LESSON VOCABULARY

about	enjoy	gives
surprise	surprised	worry
would		

INTRODUCE THE BOOK

INTRODUCE THE TITLE AND AUTHOR Discuss with children the title and the author of *Special Days, Special Food*. Based on the title, ask children what they think of when you say "special days." Their responses will often involve food, so use the opportunity to ask what they think the book will say about food.

BUILD BACKGROUND The concept underlying this reader ties special food with the good feelings that come from people's special celebrations. Have the children talk about parties on special days and the foods they associate with those parties. Talk about why food is fun to share.

PREVIEW/USE TEXT FEATURES Ask the children to look at both the illustrations and the photographs and to notice the food that people are eating. Also ask what the countries named in the headings might mean. Can they predict what this book will be about?

ELL Ask volunteers to locate their home countries on a map. Ask them to tell the class about one or two special celebrations that they enjoyed in their home country. Suggest that they describe the food they like best at a celebration and why it is part of the celebration.

READ THE BOOK

SET PURPOSE By talking about special days and food, help the children to use their own experience with these happy times to set a purpose for reading. Most children want to read happy books, and that is reason enough. Some may love to read about food, and all will want to read about parties.

STRATEGY SUPPORT: MONITOR AND FIX UP When young readers look back to find information they have forgotten or did not understand, they are helping themselves to both draw conclusions and support them. Self-questioning helps to keep children from rushing to a conclusion just as the questioning helps them to become close readers.

COMPREHENSION QUESTIONS

PAGE 4 Why do people race in boats that look like dragons on a special day in China? (*It is a way of celebrating the Dragon Boat Festival.*)

PAGE 7 What does it mean if you find a doll in your cake? (*If your piece of cake has a doll in it, you will be king or queen for the day.*)

PAGE 12 What is a recipe for? (*It helps you know how to make foods a certain way.*)

REVIST THE BOOK

THINK AND SHARE

1. Possible response: Celebrating is exciting and fun.
2. Possible responses: You can reread the text for meaning, reviewing the pictures.
3. Responses will vary.
4. Responses will vary.

EXTEND UNDERSTANDING Have students look once again at the photographs in *Special Days, Special Food*. Ask: Why are the photographs in this book so helpful? *(If the food is unfamiliar, it helps to see what it looks like.)*

RESPONSE OPTIONS

WRITING Suggest that the children make up a reason for a party day. Have them write an invitation that tells what foods and games they will be having on the special party day.

SOCIAL STUDIES CONNECTION

Time For
SOCIAL
STUDIES

Foods are a good way for people to get to know one another. This reader shows how people in many countries like to celebrate together, and a big part of celebrations involves certain foods. Make a mural market of foods that are important to all the families represented by the children in the class.

Skill Work

TEACH/REVIEW VOCABULARY

Have children examine the sentences in the reader in which the words *surprise* and *surprised* appear. Ask children to use context clues to tell how the words are alike and different. Have children locate the sentences in which the other vocabulary words appear and ask them to use context clues to offer definitions.

TARGET SKILL AND STRATEGY

DRAW CONCLUSIONS Remind children that to *draw a conclusion,* they should look at what they have read, including illustrations, and also rely on their own knowledge. Say: "I read that *zong zi* are rice balls, and that some *zong zi* are filled with meat. I know that dishes with meat usually taste salty. So I would guess that *zong zis* that are filled with meat are salty."

MONITOR AND FIX UP Remind children that what they read should make sense to them. If it doesn't, children need to identify where the difficulty is. Encourage children to periodically ask themselves questions, such as "What is the author telling us?" or "Do I understand this?" Have children go back and reread what they don't understand. Monitoring their reading will help them to draw some conclusions about the facts presented.

ADDITIONAL SKILL INSTRUCTION

AUTHOR'S PURPOSE Ask: Why do you think the author wrote this book? Are there parts where you learned something? What were those parts, and what did you learn? Did you enjoy reading this book? Which parts did you enjoy the most?

Name _____

Draw Conclusions

Read the beginning of a sentence in the left column.
Draw a line to the conclusion that makes the best ending to
that sentence.

1. On special days, people

2. At the Dragon Boat
   Festival, zong zis are
   fun because

3. In France, you get a
   doll if

4. In Cuba, it looks like
   everyone likes fruit
   because

5. In Mexico, a party is
   called a fiesta because

you find it in your piece
of cake.

they make colorful
shakes out of it.

love to make and eat
special foods.

you have to eat them to
find out what's inside.

there are many foods,
dancing, and music.

Name _____

Vocabulary

Read each sentence. Choose the word from the word box that best fits each sentence.

> **Words to Know**
>
> about   enjoy   gives   surprise
> surprised   worry   would

1. Parties and festivals are always _____ food.

2. Have you ever been _____ by food?

3. Someone _____ the winner a crown.

4. Do you ever _____ about having a party?

5. Everyone just wants to _____ special days.

6. The Cake for a King has a _____ in it.

7. _____ everyone come and help?

The Art Show

SUMMARY Matt works hard on a portrait, only to have it ruined by his baby brother. His mother persuades him to enter the picture in an art show, with surprising results.

LESSON VOCABULARY

colors	draw	drew	great
over	show	sign	

INTRODUCE THE BOOK

INTRODUCE THE TITLE AND AUTHOR Discuss the title and author of *The Art Show*. Ask children to describe what they think this book might be about, based on the title and the cover illustration. Have them share experiences they have had taking part in or attending an art show.

BUILD BACKGROUND Discuss portraits with children. Ask what artists might do to try to show the person they are drawing. Have them also talk about what happens when toddlers use crayons without anyone watching them. Have children think about whether there is just one good way to make a piece of art, or whether art may take different forms.

PREVIEW/TAKE A PICTURE WALK Invite children to take a picture walk to preview the text and illustrations. Discuss who the story will be about and what the character is drawing. Have them make guesses about the relationship between the boy and the baby shown on page 6.

ELL Display a series of paintings or drawings for children. Hold up one at a time as you use the word *picture* to describe it. Point out a large display of pictures in the classroom or the school and use the words *art show* to describe the collection.

READ THE BOOK

SET PURPOSE After children have previewed the pictures in the book, have them set a purpose for reading *The Art Show*. Ask them to think about how they might feel if they made a picture and entered it into an art show. They might read to find out if the main character feels the same way.

STRATEGY SUPPORT: VISUALIZE Tell children that good readers try to picture story events and details in their minds as they read. Explain that they can use senses such as touch and hearing, as well as sight, as they picture the events. Model the strategy: As I read pages 4 and 5, I try to picture in my mind the things that Matt may see, hear, and feel. I picture him talking with his mom and sitting down for lunch. I can almost smell and taste the peanut butter he puts on some bread.

COMPREHENSION QUESTIONS

PAGE 3 Why was Matt pleased with his work at first? (*The picture looked just like Sam; Matt loved his brother and thought about him carefully as he drew.*)

PAGES 6–7 What did Sam do to upset Matt? (*He scribbled all over Matt's drawing and colored in the wrong parts.*)

PAGE 11 What surprise did Matt get at the end of the story? (*The picture of Sam won a ribbon at the art show.*)

REVISIT THE BOOK

THINK AND SHARE

1. Possible response: A piece of art does not need to look perfect to be good.
2. Responses may vary, but should convey the idea that visualizing the scribbled picture helped children understand that Matt thought the picture was ruined.
3. Possible response: (page 9) Signs show people where to go and keep them out of danger.
4. Children should complete the web with examples of events that turned out in a surprising way, or events that helped them learn a new way to think about something.

EXTEND UNDERSTANDING Explain that readers can often understand characters in a story by thinking about what the characters say. Reread Matt's dialogue on pages 5 and 7 with expression. Discuss with children how Matt feels at these points in the story.

RESPONSE OPTIONS

WORD WORK Help children expand their familiarity with color names by having them use appropriate crayons or markers to make a color key for the words *red*, *blue*, *yellow*, *green*, *orange*, *purple*, *black*, *brown*, and *white*.

ART CONNECTION

Provide several portraits for children to look at. If possible, include photographs, illustrations, and paintings. Try to include some abstract portraits as well as ones that are realistic. Have children select one portrait and draw a picture of it. Have them write a sentence telling why they like it.

Skill Work

TEACH/REVIEW VOCABULARY

Prepare a set of vocabulary flash cards for each child. Have children make a simple drawing on the back of each card to help them recall the word's meaning. Children can work with partners to quiz each other on reading and defining the words.

TARGET SKILL AND STRATEGY

THEME Remind children that a *theme* is a "big idea" or a lesson that a story teaches. Briefly discuss the themes of other familiar stories children have read. Then have them talk about what *The Art Show* teaches them or what Matt learns.

VISUALIZE Remind children that when they *visualize*, they use story details and pictures to help them form a picture in their mind. Paying attention to the pictures and words will help them imagine and understand the story better. Ask children to share some details they pictured as they read the story.

ADDITIONAL SKILL INSTRUCTION

DRAW CONCLUSION Remind children that writers do not always tell everything about a character. Sometimes readers must use story and picture clues and what they know from real life to figure out more. Ask children to form a conclusion about how Matt feels about his picture at the end of the story. Discuss the clues and experiences that led them to this conclusion.

Name _____

Theme

A **theme** is the big idea or a lesson the story teaches.
Fill in the boxes below to find the theme of *The Art Show*.

Beginning:
_____

_____

_____

↓

Middle:
_____

_____

_____

↓

End:
_____

_____

_____

What Matt learns:
_____

_____

_____

Name _____

Vocabulary

Write the word from the box that best fits each sentence.

Check the Words You Know
colors   draw   drew   great   over   show   sign

1. Jan likes to _____ .

2. She uses many _____ .

3. One time she _____ a picture of her dog.

4. It was a _____ picture!

5. Jan put the picture in an art _____ .

6. She wrote "My Dog" on a _____ .

7. Then she hung the sign _____ the picture.

Treasures of Our Country

SUMMARY Our country is full of special places. This nonfiction selection explains why we treasure such important landmarks as Yellowstone National Park, the Grand Canyon, Hoover Dam, and the National Mall, among others.

LESSON VOCABULARY

found	mouth
once	took
wild	

INTRODUCE THE BOOK

INTRODUCE THE TITLE AND AUTHOR Discuss with children the title and author of *Treasures of Our Country*. Have them look at the cover and identify any of the pictures they know. Ask: Why do you think the word "treasure" in the title goes with these pictures?

BUILD BACKGROUND Ask children to share what they know about the Statue of Liberty, Mount Rushmore, the National Mall, or the Grand Canyon. Ask: Why do you think these places are famous?

PREVIEW/TAKE A PICTURE WALK Have children look at the photos and read the labels. Ask whether any of these places look familiar. If so, ask them what they know about a particular place.

READ THE BOOK

SET PURPOSE Have children set a purpose for reading *Treasures of Our Country* Remind children of what they discussed when the title and author were introduced. Invite them to complete this sentence: I really want to know about

_____.

STRATEGY SUPPORT: IMPORTANT IDEAS Remind children that they will read many ideas in a story. Some ideas are more important than others. *Important ideas* tell more about the main idea. Have children look for important ideas as they read.

ELL Point out these key terms from the text that may be unfamiliar to children: *hot spring, canyon, dam, monument, memorial, arch, liberty*. Restate and explain these words to support comprehension.

COMPREHENSION QUESTIONS

PAGE 5 How was the Grand Canyon formed? *(Over time, a river wore away the ground and made a deep hole.)*

PAGE 8 Name 2 facts about Mount Rushmore. *(The mouth on each face is big. These men were our leaders, and they helped our country grow.)*

PAGE 9 What monuments and memorials can be found on the National Mall in Washington, D.C.? *(the Washington Monument, the Jefferson Memorial, and the Lincoln Memorial)*

PAGE 10 If you don't know what the word *arch* means, what is one way you can find out its meaning? *(look up the definition in a dictionary)*

REVISIT THE BOOK

THINK AND SHARE

1. It lets people cross water. It has strong wires. It took 14 years to build.
2. I learned that there are treasures all around the country. It helped me to identify treasures as I read.
3. Possible response: *Wild* means living in nature.
4. Responses will vary.

EXTEND UNDERSTANDING Guide children to use the labels on page 12 to identify other national treasures not already described in the book.

RESPONSE OPTIONS

WRITING Have children write a few sentences describing one of the national treasures that they have visited, or would like to visit. Have them illustrate their description.

SOCIAL STUDIES CONNECTION

Have children do guided Internet research to find more national treasures. Provide an outline map of the United States and help children mark where each of these treasures can be found.

Skill Work

TEACH/REVIEW VOCABULARY

Give sets of vocabulary word cards to pairs of children. Also give them cards with these riddles: "If you find me, I am this." "I am less than twice." "I am like a lion." "I am on your face". "I sound like look." Have children pair words and riddles.

TARGET SKILL AND STRATEGY

FACTS AND DETAILS Tell children that *facts* and *details* support the main idea of a book. The main idea of this book is that there are many places in our country that people think are treasures. Details such as what can be found in each place help explain this idea. So do facts—things that can be proved true—such as how long it took to build the Brooklyn Bridge. Ask children to find three details or facts in the book and read them aloud.

IMPORTANT IDEAS Tell children that *important ideas* are the facts and details that tell them more about the main idea. Ask: What is the main idea of *Treasures of Our Country*? What important ideas tell more about it?

ADDITIONAL SKILL INSTRUCTION

CAUSE AND EFFECT Remind children that as they read or listen, they should think about things that happen and why those things happen. Demonstrate cause and effect by rolling a ball. Ask: What happened to the ball? *(It rolled.)* Why did this happen? *(You pushed it.)* Ask children to ask themselves what happened and why it happened as they read *Treasure Hunt!*

Name _____

Facts and Details

A *detail* is a piece of information about a story.
A *fact* is a piece of information that can be proven to be true.

I. Read the story.

> My family visited the Gateway Arch in St. Louis, Missouri,
> last summer. It is 630 feet tall. It took two years to build. We
> rode a tram to the top of the arch. There are many visitors to
> the Gateway Arch.

Read the details.
Circle the details or facts that are from the story.

a. There are many visitors to the Gateway Arch.

b. My family visited the Gateway Arch in St. Louis, Missouri,
   last summer.

c. Next summer, my family wants to visit Niagara Falls.

d. We rode a tram to the top of the arch.

2. Write one fact from the story.

_____

_____

_____

Name _____

Vocabulary

Write a word from the box that best fits into each sentence.

Words to Know
found   mouth   once   took   wild

_____

1. _____ we went to see the Grand Canyon.

_____

2. _____ animals live in Yellowstone National Park.

_____

3. I _____ a picture of Mount Rushmore.

_____

4. After looking at a map, the family _____ the Lincoln Memorial.

_____

5. At Mount Rushmore, the _____ on each face is big.

A Visit to the Ranch

SUMMARY Lia is excited to show her city cousin Maria around the ranch where she lives. After discovering how different life on a ranch is from life in the city, Maria invites Lia to visit her next summer.

LESSON VOCABULARY

above	eight
laugh	moon
touch	

INTRODUCE THE BOOK

INTRODUCE THE TITLE AND AUTHOR Discuss the title and author of *A Visit to the Ranch*. Ask children to describe what they think this book might be about, based on the title and the cover illustration. Ask children about some things they might expect to see or do on a ranch.

BUILD BACKGROUND Have children who have visited a ranch or learned about ranches describe some of the animals and activities that take place there. Discuss with children how ranches are similar to or different from the place they live.

PREVIEW/TAKE A PICTURE WALK Invite children to take a picture walk to preview the text and illustrations. Discuss what the girls are doing or thinking about on each page.

READ THE BOOK

SET PURPOSE Have children set a purpose for reading *A Visit to the Ranch*. You might suggest that they think about what each girl is discovering about where her cousin lives.

STRATEGY SUPPORT: QUESTIONING Tell children that good readers ask themselves questions as they read. They pause to make sure they understand, they ask themselves questions about the parts they do not understand, and they look for answers to their questions as they read. Model questions to ask while reading: What does this mean? Do I understand this part? Does the story answer a question I have?

COMPREHENSION QUESTIONS

PAGE 3 Why was Maria probably afraid to touch the horse? *(It was big; she had probably never seen a real horse up close before.)*

PAGE 6 Lia has never visited a city. What are some things she has probably never done? *(Possible response: gone to a museum; ridden a bike or walked a dog in a park)*

PAGE 11 What are some of the things Maria will probably write about in a letter to her family? *(Possible response: She might tell about riding a horse and describe the animals she has seen.)*

REVISIT THE BOOK

THINK AND SHARE

1. **Facts:** Cousin Maria is visiting and she has never visited the ranch before. **Details:** They rode horses; they talk about the ranch; Maria talks about city life; they rest by a stream; they wade.
2. Answers will vary.
3. Possible response: eight; My dog had eight puppies.
4. Responses will vary, but should include details to support the child's choice.

EXTEND UNDERSTANDING Ask children whether they think the characters in the story seem like real people. Discuss whether the things they do are things that could happen in real life. Ask children to support their ideas with details from the story.

RESPONSE OPTIONS

WRITING Direct children to jot down notes about things on the ranch that Maria might describe in a letter to her family. Then have them use the notes to draft a letter.

SCIENCE CONNECTION

Have children brainstorm a list of animals commonly found on a ranch or on a farm. Then explain that these animals all have a particular purpose, such as chickens producing eggs. Have children use nonfiction picture books and other sources to find out these functions. They can make a simple chart with the information they discover.

ELL Point out and write a list of concrete nouns that are pictured in the illustrations throughout *A Visit to the Ranch*. These might include words such as *fence, horse, boots, hat, calendar, bike, helmet. baseball game,* and others. Have children write each word and illustrate it in a picture dictionary.

Skill Work

TEACH/REVIEW VOCABULARY

Prepare a set of vocabulary word cards for each child. Read aloud each of the following sentences. Have children hold up the card that best completes each sentence.

1. She wanted to be brave, but she was afraid to _____ the horse. *(touch)*
2. The girls _____ at the funny story. *(laugh)*
3. Last summer, we went to _____ baseball games. *(eight)*
4. They saw the _____ rise at night. *(moon)*
5. It was in the sky _____ them. *(above)*

TARGET SKILL AND STRATEGY

FACTS AND DETAILS Tell children that facts are bits of information that can be proven to be true. Details are bits of information that tell more about important ideas in a story. Both the text and the illustrations may give details. Ask: What details in the pictures help you understand how the ranch is different from the city?

QUESTIONING Tell children that stopping to make notes about questions they have may help them focus on looking for answers as they read on.

ADDITIONAL SKILL INSTRUCTION

COMPARE AND CONTRAST Remind children that when they think about how two things are alike they are *comparing*. When they think abut how things are different, they are *contrasting*. Ask them to think about one way that life on a city is different from life on a ranch and one way it is the same.

Name _____

Facts and Details

Read each event from the story.
Circle the detail that helps you understand it.

1. Maria was afraid to touch the horse.

    She never petted a horse before.

    She liked to ride a bike.

2. The girls had fun when they waded in the water.

    They went to see the cows and sheep.

    They laughed when they got wet.

3. The girls rode all day long.

    The moon rose in the sky when they were riding.

    The girls ate dinner with Lia's family.

4. The horses waited while the girls waded in the water.

    The horses were hungry.

    The girls tied good knots.

5. Maria asked Lia to visit her.

    Lia said city life sounded like fun.

    Lia rode horses all the time.

Name _____

Vocabulary

Write a word from the box next to the correct meaning.

Words to Know
eight   moon   above   touch   laugh

1. _____ what you do when something is funny

2. _____ something that is in the sky at night

3. _____ a number that is one more than seven

4. _____ what you do when you pet something

5. _____ opposite of below

Draw something that makes you laugh. Write about it.

My Little Brother Drew

SUMMARY In this humorous story, a young girl learns how to help take care of her baby brother.

LESSON VOCABULARY

picture	remember
room	stood
thought	

INTRODUCE THE BOOK

INTRODUCE THE TITLE AND AUTHOR Discuss with children the title and author of *My Little Brother Drew*. Have children look at the cover picture. Who do they think Sue and Drew are? What do they notice about what the little boy is doing? How do they think the girl is feeling? What do they think they might find out about the children?

BUILD BACKGROUND Define *toddler* for the class. Then, have children share their knowledge of, and experience with, toddlers. Do they think it would be easy to take care of a toddler? Why or why not?

PREVIEW Invite children to look through the book before reading. Ask them what the little boy is doing and how the girl is reacting. Then ask what children think the parents are doing. Based on the preview, what do children think the story will be about?

ELL Help children to define *thought* and *remember*. Give examples of word usage. Then, have children go through the illustrations and point to the pictures that illustrate the rest of the vocabulary words.

READ THE BOOK

SET PURPOSE Have children set a purpose for reading *My Little Brother Drew*. To help guide children, look at page 3. Ask them if they want to find out why Sue is chasing Drew around. Or, perhaps, they want to learn why Sue is sitting in Drew's room at the end of the book.

STRATEGY SUPPORT: STORY STRUCTURE Remind children that stories are arranged in an order from beginning to end. Each event in the story leads to the next. When they think about how all these events fit together, they can tell what the story is all about. Explain to children that the author set up *My Little Brother Drew* in three parts. All three parts have to do with the problem Sue has in the story. In Part 1, we learn who the characters are and what the problem is. In Part 2, we see how Sue tries to stop Drew from doing things the wrong way. In Part 3, we find out that Sue now knows how to solve the problem. Have children identify these three parts as they read.

COMPREHENSION QUESTIONS

PAGE 4 How do you think Sue is feeling? *(Possible response: frustrated)*

PAGE 5 Sue is now smiling in the picture. What happened to make her happy? *(Possible response: She found a way to deal with Drew.)*

PAGE 6 Look at what is happening in the picture. Could this really happen? *(yes)*

PAGE 11 What time of day is it when the story ends? Do you think that is a good time for the story to end? Why or why not? *(nighttime; responses will vary.)*

REVISIT THE BOOK

THINK AND SHARE

1. Possible response: Sue learns how to help Drew do things.
2. Possible response: Beginning: Sue thinks Drew is always getting into trouble. Middle: Sue's parents tell Sue to show Drew how to do things the right way. End: Sue knows how to make Drew fall asleep.
3. Possible responses: zoom, boom, loom
4. Responses will vary.

EXTEND UNDERSTANDING Invite children to think about how they would feel if they were Sue. Would they enjoy teaching a toddler new things or would they be frustrated? Do they think Sue likes being a big sister? Why or why not?

RESPONSE OPTIONS

WRITING Ask children to think about something that is important for a young child to learn. Then, have children write a few sentences about what that thing is and why it is important. Children can draw a picture to illustrate their ideas.

MUSIC CONNECTION

Give children the opportunity to listen to a variety of music at a listening center. Music should include classical, kid music, and appropriate contemporary music. Invite children to decide which music they would pick for a toddler. Afterward, discuss reasons for the choices.

Skill Work

TEACH/REVIEW VOCABULARY

Create vocabulary word cards. Divide the words into nouns (*picture, room*) and verbs (*stood, thought, remember*). Have children pick a verb card and a noun card and use both words together in a sentence.

TARGET SKILL AND STRATEGY

THEME Remind children that the *theme* is the "big idea" or lesson they can learn from a story. Thinking about what the story is mostly about can help readers find the theme. As children read *My Little Brother Drew*, ask: What is this story mostly about? What lesson do you think the author wants us to learn?

STORY STRUCTURE Remind children that each event in a story leads to the next event. Together, these events show what the story is all about. Ask: What do we learn about Drew in the beginning of the story? *(he gets into a lot of things)* What does Sue first do when she sees Drew doing something wrong? *(she asks her parents for help)* What do Sue's parents tell her to do? *(show Drew the right way to do things)* What does Sue learn in the end *(she knows how to teach Drew new things)*

ADDITIONAL SKILL INSTRUCTION

REALISM AND FANTASY Invite children to think of stories where make-believe events occurred. Then, have children think of examples of stories where the events could happen. Afterward, look through *My Little Brother Drew,* stopping at each picture to ask if it shows something that could really happen. If needed, point out that even though the pictures are funny and don't show real people, the events in the story could really happen.

Name _____

Theme

Circle the sentence that best answers the question.

1. What is *My Little Brother Drew* mostly about?

   Drew gets very messy when he eats.

   Sue learns how to help Drew do things.

   Drew learns how to pull down drapes.

2. What is the "big idea" or lesson of this story?

   Showing how to do something is the best way to teach.

   Showing how to do something makes Drew more messy.

   Showing how to do something helps Drew go to sleep.

3. Think of how Sue helps Drew in the story.
   Draw a picture of Sue helping Drew learn to do something new.

Name _____

Vocabulary

Unscramble the words below and then use each one in a sentence.

Words to Know				
picture	remember	room	stood	thought

1. oodts

_____

_____

_____

2. tpiucer

_____

_____

_____

3. moro

_____

_____

_____

4. hgtouht

_____

_____

_____

5. memrereb

_____

_____

_____

The Story of the Kids Care Club

SUMMARY This nonfiction reader explains the beginning of a nationwide program called Kids Care Club. The club is made up of kids who like to volunteer in their neighborhoods and cities. The reader explores some ways kids can make their world better by helping others.

LESSON VOCABULARY

across	because
dance	only
opened	shoes
told	

INTRODUCE THE BOOK

INTRODUCE THE TITLE AND AUTHOR Ask children to look at the front cover of the reader. Show them the title of the book, and the author's name.

BUILD BACKGROUND Ask children if they have ever done something to help a neighbor or stranger. Ask them to give some examples. Then invite the children to discuss how it made them feel to help others.

PREVIEW/ILLUSTRATIONS Invite children to open the book and take a picture walk through the book. Then ask: Does this story look like it could really happen? There are a lot of people in the illustrations, but ask the children if they can tell who the main characters are.

READ THE BOOK

SET PURPOSE After children have previewed the book, ask them what question(s) they want to be able to answer after they read the book. If the children don't suggest it, then ask if they would like to know why the characters in the pictures are doing so much work.

STRATEGY SUPPORT: PREDICT/CONFIRM PREDICTIONS While children are reading, have them pause after each page and think about what they have read. Have them use that information to *predict* what might happen next. Remind them to check their predictions to see whether they were correct. Encourage them to reread to see why their predictions may have been incorrect.

COMPREHENSION QUESTIONS

PAGE 3 Is this a true story? *(Yes)*

PAGE 4 What is the cause and what is the effect on this page? *(They raked an old woman's yard; she was happy and surprised.)*

PAGE 5 Why did the children like helping people? *(It made people happy.)*

PAGE 6 Is there only one Kids Care Club? *(No)*

PAGE 10 Does the Kids Care Club only help older people? *(No, it helps kids too.)*

REVISIT THE BOOK

THINK AND SHARE

1. Kids wanted to make their neighborhood a better place. Other kids across the country opened Kids Care Clubs.
2. Responses will vary, but might include that the club would grow.
3. *helpful, lonely;* sentences will vary.
4. Responses will vary, but might include that the kids help others in ways such as visiting old people and feeding the poor.

EXTEND UNDERSTANDING Two different things are happening in the picture on page 9. Ask children to identify those two things. *(A boy is taking food to a man in a wheelchair, and an older woman is showing children photos from a box.)*

RESPONSE OPTIONS

WRITING Write the vocabulary words on the board and ask children to write a sentence using one of them.

SOCIAL STUDIES CONNECTION

Time For SOCIAL STUDIES

Invite children to discuss something they would like to do that would be helpful to their community. Ask the children to decide as a group (vote by raising of hands, if necessary). Then help them follow through with the task.

Skill Work

TEACH/REVIEW VOCABULARY

Write the vocabulary words on the board. As the children read the book, pause for the vocabulary words. Ask the children what they think the words mean, and provide the clarification or the right answers when needed.

ELL Ask English language learners to discuss some ways they could help people in their city or town. Ask them to draw a picture illustrating one of the ideas.

TARGET SKILL AND STRATEGY

CAUSE AND EFFECT Explain to children that a *cause* is something that happens, and an *effect* is something that happens as a result of the cause. Give children a couple of examples that they can relate to. (Some examples: Cause: You spend the whole day playing in the hot sun; Effect: You get a sunburn. Cause: There is a very bad snowstorm; Effect: There is a "snow day" and school is cancelled.) Ask children to discuss the causes and effects discussed in *The Story of the Kids Care Club*.

PREDICT/CONFIRM PREDICTIONS Remind children to look for clues that help them decide what might happen next. After reading pages 3–5, have them think about what the types of activities the Kids Care Club might do. Make a chart on the board listing their predictions and the support for their predictions. After they have finished reading the book, review the chart to identify whether or not their predictions were correct.

ADDITIONAL SKILL INSTRUCTION

AUTHOR'S PURPOSE After reading the book, explain to the children that the author's purpose is the reason why the author wrote the book. Invite the children to turn to page 12 and read the last sentence. Explain that the author wanted to tell the children about the club so that they could start one if it sounded fun.

Name _____

Cause and Effect

Circle the best answer for each question below.

1. Why did the kids rake their neighbor's lawn?

   The kids did not like to rake leaves.

   The neighbor could not rake the leaves herself.

   The neighbor was not nice to them.

2. Why did the kids make 150 lunches?

   The kids were very hungry.

   The kids wanted to sell the lunches.

   Some people did not have enough to eat.

3. Why did the children join the Kids Care Club?

   Kids wanted to help others.

   Kids wanted to make sandwiches.

   Kids wanted to earn money.

4. Why do Kids Care Clubs visit older people?

   The kids are lonely.

   The older people are tired.

   The older people are lonely.

5. Why does the Kids Care Club collect clothes and shoes?

   so that they could give them to children in need

   so that they could keep them for themselves

   so that they could throw them away

Name _____

Vocabulary

Draw a line to match the word with its meaning.

1. across	a. not more than; just
2. because	b. to move to music
3. dance	c. from one side to another side
4. only	d. not closed
5. opened	e. for the reason that
6. shoes	f. a covering for feet
7. told	g. to say (past tense)

Squirrel and Bear

SUMMARY In this story, a squirrel wants to eat a farmer's pumpkin instead of his own apples, but the pumpkin is too large to move. The problem is solved when he gets help from a bear, who is rewarded with the squirrel's apples. The story supports the lesson concept that some problems need clever solutions.

LESSON VOCABULARY

along	behind
eyes	never
pulling	toward

INTRODUCE THE BOOK

INTRODUCE THE TITLE AND AUTHOR Discuss with children the title and author of *Squirrel and Bear*. Also have children look at the picture on the cover. Tell children that science is the study of nature and the world around us. Based on the title and picture, ask: How might this story have something to do with science?

BUILD BACKGROUND Ask children to share what they know about the things that animals eat. Ask: Do animals ever eat what we eat? Do they ever eat each other?

PREVIEW Have children preview by looking at the pictures in the book. Ask: Who is this story mostly about? What happens at the beginning of the story? Have children read the heading on page 12. Ask and discuss: Is this page part of the story? Do you think this page is about something real, or something made up?

READ THE BOOK

SET PURPOSE Have children set a purpose for reading *Squirrel and Bear*. Discuss what apples and pumpkins look like and feel like. Ask: Do you eat apples? pumpkin pie? What do they taste like? As children read, ask them to think about whether real bears and squirrels like to eat apples and pumpkins.

STRATEGY SUPPORT: MONITOR AND CLARIFY

Remind children that good readers know that what they read must make sense. Tell children that they should check as they read this book to make sure they understand what they are reading. Model questions to ask while reading: What does this mean? Does this make sense? Do I understand this? Model by reading pages 3 and 4. Say: This doesn't make a lot of sense. The picture on page 4 shows Squirrel holding a pumpkin, but I know that pumpkins are way too heavy for squirrels to lift. I will read on to see if the story explains how this is possible. After reading page 6, say: Now I understand. The pumpkin *is* too heavy for Squirrel. The picture on page 4 must be showing what Squirrel thought would happen.

ELL Point out the words *scowled* on page 3, and *peeked* and *greetings* on page 8. Restate, act out, and explain these words for less-proficient speakers.

COMPREHENSION QUESTIONS

PAGE 3 Where was Squirrel? *(in his apple tree)*

PAGE 6 What are the three different ways that Squirrel tried to move the pumpkin? *(He tried lifting it, he tried pushing it, and he tried pulling it.)*

PAGE 8 Squirrel said hello to Bear. Could this really happen, or is it make-believe? Why? *(It is make-believe because animals can't talk in real life.)*

PAGES 9–10 What happened after Squirrel spoke to Bear? *(Bear pushed the pumpkin to Squirrel's tree.)*

PAGE 11 Suppose this story happened in a house. How would you change the characters and the plot? *(Possible response: I would have a mouse ask a cat for help to move a slice of cake.)*

REVISIT THE BOOK

THINK AND SHARE

1. Setting: in a tree; in a pumpkin patch
   Characters: Squirrel and Bear
   What happened: Squirrel wants a pumpkin.
   He is too small to move it. Squirrel sees
   Bear. Bear says she likes apples. Squirrel
   gives Bear apples and Bear moves the pumpkin for Squirrel.
2. Responses will vary.
3. Drawings will vary.
4. Responses will vary.

EXTEND UNDERSTANDING Turn children's attention to the background information on page
12. Ask: How do wild animals get their food?
How do farm animals get their food? How
do pets get their food? How do you get your
food? Guide children to see that animals in
the wild must get their own food from where
they live.

RESPONSE OPTIONS

WRITING Suggest that children pretend that
they are the farmer who owns the pumpkin
patch. Have them write three sentences
about what the farmer might say to Squirrel.
Encourage children to think about why the
farmer grows pumpkins.

SCIENCE CONNECTION

Display books and other information about different animals
and what they eat. Have children
choose an animal and draw it and the food it
typically eats. Have them include the typical
landscape in which the animal lives.

Skill Work

TEACH/REVIEW VOCABULARY

Give each child a set of vocabulary word
cards. Say one of these phrases, one by
one, and have children hold up the word that
best matches the phrase: *not in front, things
to see with, not even sometimes, also with,
to the way of, dragging away.*

TARGET SKILL AND STRATEGY

CHARACTER, SETTING, AND PLOT Tell children that *characters* are people or animals
in the story. The *setting* is where the story
takes place, and the *plot* is what happens
in the story. Discuss how characters often
learn things in the course of the story. Tell
children that Squirrel is the main character
in the story. As children read, they should
think about how Squirrel gets the pumpkin
and what he learns. Then, to help children
focus on setting, point out the story takes
place in a tree and a pumpkin patch.

MONITOR AND CLARIFY Remind children to
stop and clarify if they don't understand what
they are reading. Model questions to ask:
What does this mean? Do I understand this?
Explain to children that reading on in a story
might help answer some of their questions. As
they read, ask children to share some of their
questions about the story. Have them read on
in the story to see if they can answer it.

ADDITIONAL SKILL INSTRUCTION

REALISM AND FANTASY Explain to children
that both realistic stories and fantasies can
be made-up stories. The difference is that
the former could happen in real life and the
other could not. Encourage children to ask
themselves these questions as they read:
Do the people and animals do what real
people and animals do? Are there things in
the story that could not really happen?
Do animals talk in the story? Is there magic
in the story? Have children write down anything that happens in the story that could
not happen in real life.

Name _____

Character, Setting, and Plot

A **character** is the person or animal that the story is about. The **setting** is the "where and when" of the story. The **plot** describes what happens in the story.

Think of something else Bear could help Squirrel move.
Then draw a picture of Bear helping Squirrel.
Under your picture, write what is happening, where Squirrel and Bear are, and how Squirrel feels.

Name _____

Vocabulary

Write the word from the box that best fits each sentence.

never	pulling	toward
behind	along	eyes

_____

1. I stood in line _____ Ann and in front of Dave.

_____

2. You should _____ ride a bike without a helmet.

_____

3. A face has two _____, one nose, and one mouth.

_____

4. Try _____ the door to open it.

5. Write three words from the Word Box that describe where you might find something.

_____

_____

_____

Puppy Raiser

SUMMARY Through the fictional characters of Sally and her mother, the children learn about puppy raisers in this informational book. Raising a puppy to be a guide dog involves giving the puppy love, training the dog, exposing it to many people, and helping it get used to traveling. Because Sally is good at all those things, her mother thinks she will make a good puppy raiser.

LESSON VOCABULARY

door	loved
should	wood

INTRODUCE THE BOOK

INTRODUCE THE TITLE AND AUTHOR Discuss with children the title and the author of *Puppy Raiser*. Based on the title and cover illustration, ask children if they know what they will be reading about. If any of the children have or had puppies, talk about whether they think this will be a book just like the experiences they had or if there might be something different about this book.

BUILD BACKGROUND Introduce the children to the idea that, while many of us may have raised puppies to adult dogs, this is a book about raising puppies to be guide dogs. Discuss what children know of guide dogs, where they may have seen them, and what purpose they serve.

PREVIEW/TAKE A PICTURE WALK By looking at the illustrations and photos in this book, see what ideas the children have about these special puppies. Ask what things they see in the photos that make these puppies different.

READ THE BOOK

SET PURPOSE Go back to how you introduced the book, its title and author and ask children to set their own purpose for reading this book about guide dogs. Most children love puppies, which can be reason enough, and some may be especially interested in how dogs can be trained to help humans.

STRATEGY SUPPORT: BACKGROUND KNOWLEDGE Remind children that they can use their own experiences to help them understand what they read. Model a text-to-self connection on page 3: This reminds me of a dog I saw last spring. The dog in the picture looks more well-behaved, though.

COMPREHENSION QUESTIONS

PAGE 3 Why are guide dogs introduced at the beginning of this book? *(because puppy raisers raise dogs to be guide dogs)*

PAGES 6, 10 What is the first and last things Sally knew about being a puppy raiser? *(first, to give them love; last, to give them back)*

PAGE 8 Why does a guide dog need its owner to take it many places? *(so it will get used to different people)*

PAGE 9 If a guide dog goes in cars, trains, and buses, what will it be able to do? *(It will be able to travel with its new owner.)*

PAGE 11 How was Sally going to be able to give up a puppy? *(She knew it was going to someone who needs it.)*

PAGE 12 Why was Sally's mother going to let her be a puppy raiser? *(She was good at doing each of the necessary things to raise the puppy.)*

REVISIT THE BOOK

THINK AND SHARE

1. Possible responses: Being a puppy raiser takes a lot of hard work.; Being a puppy raiser is very rewarding.
2. Answers will vary.
3. Sentences will vary.
4. Responses will vary.

EXTEND UNDERSTANDING Help the children see that the story of Sally and her mother is a fiction, or made-up, part of this text. The made-up part is used to help inform the reader about raising puppies to be guide dogs. Discuss why they think the author described puppy raising by using a child to tell the steps. Suggest that they write or draw a cartoon story using a character to describe the steps of doing an activity they know well.

RESPONSE OPTIONS

WRITING Encourage the children to continue the activity suggested above in *Extend Understanding*. Help them to make the steps in the activity clear by listing them first before beginning their story.

SOCIAL STUDIES CONNECTION

Time For SOCIAL STUDIES

Using the story of Sally becoming a puppy raiser as an example, ask the children to write one sentence about one thing they would like to do to help people at home, or at school, or in the neighborhood. Put the sentences up as part of a "We are citizens who help" display.

Skill Work

TEACH/REVIEW VOCABULARY

To give the children practice in recognizing the diphthong *ou*, place these sentences on the board and ask the children to underline the diphthong as they say the word. *James would not cut the wood. Children should go to school. Should you open the door? Puppies should be loved.* Talk about how *oo* and *ou* can sound alike in *would* and *wood* and how they sound different in *door* and *would*.

ELL Spend some time distinguishing the diphthong with children who may have difficulty learning the spelling of *should* and *wood*, despite their similarity in sound.

TARGET SKILL AND STRATEGY

DRAW CONCLUSIONS Model: On page 3, the text says that guide dogs help people who cannot see. The picture shows a dog on a special leash. I know that dogs can be trained to sit and walk on command. Based on what I see and what I know, I think these dogs help people by walking and stopping. The special leash the person holds helps them learn from the dog when it is safe to walk across a street or when they should stop and wait. After children read page 12, ask: Do you think Sally's mother allows Sally to be a puppy raiser? Why?

BACKGROUND KNOWLEDGE Explain to children that what they already know can be from experiences they've had, from reading, or from things other people have taught them. After reading, ask: Have you ever helped train a puppy? Have you ever read any stories about guide dogs? How did that help you when you read this story about puppy raisers?

ADDITIONAL SKILL INSTRUCTION

MAIN IDEA In this book, the children are dealing with the big idea of guide dogs and how they are raised in a special way. To start the discussion, ask: "What was *Puppy Raiser* all about?" Encourage two or three word answers, but saying only the word "puppies" does not show an understanding of the *main idea*. Accept any responses the children have that contains the idea of raising puppies to be guide dogs.

Name _____

Draw Conclusions

Use what you read in the book and what you already know to circle the answers to these questions. Each question will have more than one answer.

1. What do you need to be in order to be a good puppy raiser?

   caring   friendly   fast

2. In what ways can guide dogs help people?

   cross the street   listen to music   travel

3. What kinds of places might a guide dog go with an owner?

   to work   to school   to a restaurant

Now, draw two conclusions about guide dogs.

   _____
   ----

4. Guide dogs are _____

   _____
   ----

   and _____ .

Name _____

Vocabulary

Pick a word from the box to finish each sentence.
Write it on the line.

Words to Know
door   loved   should   wood

1. A dog _____ always obey.

2. Pets need to feel _____.

3. My desk is made of _____.

4. Close the _____ when you leave.

A Mighty Oak Tree

SUMMARY This nonfiction reader offers information about the life of an oak tree—how fast or tall it grows, how long it lives, where it grows, who lives in it, and so on. It includes amazing facts about oak trees and compares oaks to other types of trees.

LESSON VOCABULARY

among	another
instead	none

INTRODUCE THE BOOK

INTRODUCE THE TITLE AND AUTHOR Discuss with children the title and author of *A Mighty Oak Tree*. Based on the title, ask children what kind of information they think this book will provide. Ask: Do you recognize the tree on the cover? Does it look like a tree in your neighborhood?

BUILD BACKGROUND Discuss what children know about oak trees. Discuss what children know about trees in general. If possible, bring children to the window of the classroom and point out various types of trees. Ask: Does anyone know what an oak leaf looks like?

PREVIEW/TAKE A PICTURE WALK Have children look at the photos in the book. Ask: What do you learn from the photos? Encourage children to share knowledge they already have about trees in relation to the photos. For page 10, ask: Have you ever seen animals living in trees? Have you ever seen squirrels with acorns?

ELL Pair less-proficient speakers with more-proficient speakers and have them discuss the photos and the captions in the book. Encourage children to discuss what they see happening in and around trees in their own yards.

READ THE BOOK

SET PURPOSE As children preview the text, have them set a purpose for reading. Ask: What do you want to know about oak trees and other trees?

STRATEGY SUPPORT: MONITOR AND CLARIFY Remind children that you *monitor* your reading to make sure that you understand, and if the text does not make sense, then you *clarify* your understanding. Have children periodically ask themselves, "Do I understand this?" If not, have them write down all of the information they do know from the text.

COMPREHENSION QUESTIONS

PAGE 3 How are oak trees like most trees? *(Possible response: They have leaves and branches.)*

PAGE 5 What helps oak trees grow? *(water and light)*

PAGE 6 How long can oak trees live? *(hundreds of years)*

PAGE 8 Can an oak tree live forever? *(no)*

PAGE 10 What kinds of animals live in oak trees? *(Possible responses: squirrels, birds, owls)*

PAGE 11 What are two other things you could make from an oak tree? *(Possible responses: bookcase, table)*

PAGE 11 What conclusions can you draw from this page? *(People need trees. Trees help make our lives better.)*

REVISIT THE BOOK

THINK AND SHARE

1. Possible responses:
   Animals: food, shelter
   People: shade, pretty to look at, to make furniture
2. water, sunlight
3. *growing, living, raking, planting, making, walking; grow, live, rake, plant, make, walk*
4. It is bigger.

EXTEND UNDERSTANDING Have children examine the illustrations and labels throughout the book. Help children get the most out of the illustrations. Ask: On page 3, how many branches are on the tree? Is the bark the same thing as the trunk? For pages 4 and 5, say: Oak trees drink water through their roots. Ask: Where are the roots in the pictures? Could you see them if you stood beside the house in the picture?

RESPONSE OPTIONS

WRITING Have children write a short thank-you note to trees, for example, thanking them for providing shade or for being something to climb.

WORD WORK Use finger puppets to demonstrate the definition of each word, particularly how each word shows a relationship between people or things. Name your puppets Manny, Moe, Jack, and Jill. Say: Jill is playing *among* the other puppets. Jack is on one team and Jill is on *another* team. Manny picked Jack to be on his team *instead* of Jill. *None* of the puppets want to play anymore. You may want to leave the vocabulary word blank and have the children fill in the blanks.

SCIENCE CONNECTION

Have children study seeds for different types of plants, such as acorns, peach pits, sunflowers, and dandelions. Have children draw the seeds and the plants they become.

Skill Work

TEACH/REVIEW VOCABULARY

Review the vocabulary words and definitions. Show how the letter *o* has the same sound in *among, another,* and *none.* Ask: What other words use an *o* with the sound heard in *none*? Write responses on the chalkboard. Then model how to use the vocabulary words and the children's words in a sentence. For example: *The monkey hung among the branches. None of the children won a prize.*

TARGET SKILL AND STRATEGY

COMPARE AND CONTRAST Review that to *compare* and *contrast* is to tell how things are the same and how they are different. Make a T-chart on the board listing the qualities of an oak tree and another type of tree. Fill in the list together. Then ask children: How are the two trees alike? How are they different?

MONITOR AND CLARIFY As children read, have them ask: "What does this mean?" or "Do I understand this?" Explain that this is called *monitoring* understanding. When they cannot answer those questions, tell them they can *clarify* their understanding of the text by rereading to see if they can find the answers. Explain that when reading a text like this, with a lot of new information, they should review what they have read both during and after reading.

ADDITIONAL SKILL INSTRUCTION

DRAW CONCLUSIONS Remind children to use what they read in the book and what they know about real life to figure out more about what happens in *A Mighty Oak Tree.* Show children how they can figure out things about oak trees that are not stated in the text. Help them by asking questions, such as: What happened to the oak tree that was used to make a chair? *(It was chopped down and cut up.)* How can you tell the age of an oak tree? *(by its height and width)*

Name _____

Compare and Contrast

We **compare** objects to tell how they are alike.
We **contrast** objects to tell how they are different.

Use *A Mighty Oak Tree* to answer the questions.

I. How are squirrels and deer alike?

_____

- -

_____

2. How are birds are squirrels alike?

_____

- -

_____

3. How are birds and squirrels different?

_____

- -

_____

4. How are squirrels and bears different?

_____

- -

_____

Name _____

Vocabulary

Write the word from the box that best fits each sentence.

Words to Know
among   another   instead   none

1. Squirrels live _____ other animals in the trees.

2. In some places, oak trees grow _____ of other trees.

3. That squirrel ate _____ of the acorns.

4. _____ squirrel ate all of the acorns.

5. Practice writing each of the vocabulary words on the lines.

_____   _____

_____   _____

_____   _____

Simple Machines at Work

SUMMARY Using simple pictures and text, this selection describes six different kinds of simple machines—inclined planes, wedges, screws, levers, pulleys, and wheels and axles—and explains that they are all tools that make work easier.

LESSON VOCABULARY

against	goes
heavy	kinds
today	

INTRODUCE THE BOOK

INTRODUCE THE TITLE AND AUTHOR Discuss with students the title and the author of *Simple Machines at Work*. Based on the title, ask students to describe the image they get of what the book will be about—especially before they look at the photographs. Ask students why they think the content triangle says *Science*. Ask: What other science books have children read?

BUILD BACKGROUND Make sure that students understand that machines can be simple, everyday devices. Spend a few minutes identifying simple machines that are close at hand, such as rulers, doorstops, wheels on toys, or wheelchair ramps. Ask students to recall and describe a time when they used a simple machine to help them do something.

PREVIEW/TAKE A PICTURE WALK As children preview the book, the pictures of various machines will probably attract their curiosity. Draw their attention to the use of labels in the pictures, on pages 6 and 7 for example. Ask: What does the combination of the label and the picture tell you about these machines?

READ THE BOOK

SET PURPOSE Have children set a purpose for reading *Simple Machines at Work*. Children's interest in machines, mechanical objects, or moving toys should guide this purpose. Suggest that children think of a toy whose workings they might like to understand.

STRATEGY SUPPORT: SUMMARIZE As children read, extracting the main ideas for the purpose of summarizing will help them understand and retain what they read. As an aid, if necessary, draw up a list of the six types of simple machines mentioned in this selection. Ask: What is the author's main point about these machines? What do they all do?

COMPREHENSION QUESTIONS

PAGE 3 What sentence expresses the key idea on this page? *(Simple machines help you do work with less force.)*

PAGE 7 What does a wedge do? *(It goes between two things.)*

PAGE 9 Name an object that you could use as a lever. *(Possible response: ruler or stick)*

PAGE 10 What are the two parts of a pulley? *(a wheel and something that goes around the wheel, such as a rope)*

PAGE 10 How is a pulley like a wheel and axle? *(Possible response: They both use wheels.)*

PAGE 10 Name one difference between a pulley and a wheel and axle. *(Possible response: Wheels and axles do not use ropes or chains.)*

REVISIT THE BOOK

THINK AND SHARE

1. Possible response: There are six kinds of simple machines, and they make work easier.
2. inclined plane, lever, wheel and axle; Sentences will vary.
3. Pictures and sentences will vary.
4. Possible response: The Inclined Plane

EXTEND UNDERSTANDING As children look at the pictures, ask which ones really help them understand how the machines work. Ask if any pictures make them think about a time when they used a wedge or other machine. If any-thing in the pictures confuses children, help them understand what they are seeing. Ask children to pick one machine and make their own drawing of it, including labels.

RESPONSE OPTIONS

VIEWING Have children bring in a simple machine from home, or find a simple machine used in the classroom, such as a screw-on lid. Being mindful of safety, invite children to demonstrate the use of their machine.

SCIENCE CONNECTION

TIME FOR **Science**

Have children choose one type of simple machine and make a list of every example they can find of this machine, at home and at school. Encourage them to look at their toys and com-mon household items. Invite children to share their lists with others.

Skill Work

TEACH/REVIEW VOCABULARY

To reinforce the contextual meaning of *against*, read the bottom paragraph on page 4 and then use *against* in other sentences. Continue in a similar fashion with the remaining vocabulary words.

ELL Ask English language learners to note any words in the selection they do not understand, including vocabulary words. Suggest that they look at pictures and reread for context clues. If necessary, invite them to use a dictionary or ask for the definition.

TARGET SKILL AND STRATEGY

MAIN IDEA Tell children that a *main idea* is what an article is all about. The main idea gives the gist of a selection. Guide stu-dents in identifying the main idea of *Simple Machines at Work* by asking: What do you see on every page of this article? What is the title of the selection? For first graders, a phrase such as *six simple machines* can adequately express the main idea.

SUMMARIZE Explain to children that a *summary* of an article is a brief state-ment that gives the main idea but leaves out unimportant details. Invite children to recall the important ideas of the article and restate them in their own words. Guide them in separating main ideas from supporting details. Point out, for example, that a supporting detail might be: *An ax is a kind of wedge.*

ADDITIONAL SKILL INSTRUCTION

COMPARE AND CONTRAST Tell children that to compare and contrast is to find similarities and differences between things. Draw children's attention to pages 10 and 11. To find similarities, help students make a list of descriptions that fit pulleys as well as wheels and axles. Include such descriptions as *simple machine, has two parts, helps things move, includes a wheel, requires force to work.* Now help children identify differences between the two machines.

Name _____

Main Idea

A main idea is the most important idea about a passage or group of sentences.

Read the sentences below and then write a title for this passage on the blank line.

> A ramp is a type of simple machine called an inclined plane. Inclined planes make it easier to move things up or down. The road in this picture is an inclined plane. The slide on your playground is also an inclined plane.

_____

Read the sentences below and then write a title for this passage on the blank line.

> Simple machines make work easier. A wedge is a kind of simple machine. It uses force to go between two things. A screw is also a simple machine. The lid of a jar and the bottom of a light bulb are both kinds of screws. Screws make it easier to put things together. A lever is a simple machine for pushing things up. When you push down on one end of the lever, the other end goes up.

_____

Name _____

Vocabulary

Write the word or words from the box that have the same vowel sound as each word below.

Words to Know

against   goes   heavy   kinds   today

1. find _____

2. sent _____

3. fed _____

4. play _____

5. rows _____

Look at the group of words after each bold word.
Circle the word or phrase that does not belong.

6. **against**   a. near   b. far   c. next to

7. **goes**   a. moves   b. stops   c. travels

8. **heavy**   a. feather   b. rock   c. truck

9. **kinds**   a. copies   b. types   c. brands

10. **today**   a. now   b. current   c. past

The Communication Story

SUMMARY This book tells the history of long-distance communication. It supports and extends the lesson concept that the invention of the telephone improved communication in our world.

LESSON VOCABULARY

built	early	learn
science	through	

INTRODUCE THE BOOK

INTRODUCE THE TITLE AND AUTHOR Discuss with children the title and author of *The Communication Story*. Also have children look at the picture on the cover. Say: Many scientists try to improve our world. How might this book have something to do with science?

BUILD BACKGROUND Ask children to share what they know about how people stay in touch over long distances. Ask them to tell or suggest how this was done long ago.

ELL Have children share home-language words that relate to the telephone and other forms of long-distance communication.

PREVIEW/TAKE A PICTURE WALK Have children look at the pictures in the book before reading. Say: Think about the title of this book. What do you think the people in these pictures are doing? When did these people live? What is this book about?

READ THE BOOK

SET PURPOSE Have children set a purpose for reading *The Communication Story*. Remind children of what they discussed when the title, author, and cover art were introduced. Invite them to complete this sentence: I really want to know about _____.

STRATEGY SUPPORT: TEXT STRUCTURE Explain to children that authors can organize information in a nonfiction book in a number of ways. One way is by breaking the book up into sections. Each section will tell the reader about something new. As children read, have them pay attention to how the information is broken up into sections.

COMPREHENSION QUESTIONS

PAGES 4–5 How is communicating with smoke signals different from communicating with drums? Make a list of differences. *(Possible response: Smoke signals: uses smoke, must be high up, depends on sight; Drums: uses drums, depends on sound)*

PAGE 7 When did people use horses to send the mail? *(Possible response: before trains and cars)*

PAGE 9 Do you think that the telegraph is best for sending long messages? Why or why not? *(Possible response: No. Sending messages one letter at a time is slow and the message is probably short.)*

PAGE 9 What skills would you need to send messages by telegraph? *(Possible response: good spelling, knowing the beeps, good listening)*

REVIST THE BOOK

THINK AND SHARE

1. smoke, mail, pigeons, telephone
2. Responses will vary.
3. Possible responses: I built a house. I went to bed early. I learn spelling in school. Science is my favorite subject. I went through the doorway.
4. Drawings and responses will vary.

EXTEND UNDERSTANDING Guide children to use the pictures in the book to identify when each form of communication was used and where it was used.

RESPONSE OPTIONS

WRITING Have children describe how to use a telephone or computer to communicate.

SCIENCE CONNECTION

Display information about carrier pigeons, the mail, the telegraph, the telephone, and e-mail. Have children choose one of these forms of communication and then draw a diagram that shows how a message gets sent from one point to another.

TIME FOR Science

Skill Work

TEACH/REVIEW VOCABULARY

Have children use the vocabulary words to replace one word in each sentence to best change its meaning: I forget as much as I can at school. Find the truth through dreams. My brother broke my bike. The bus came late this morning. I ran around the puddle.

TARGET SKILL AND STRATEGY

SEQUENCE Remind children that *sequence* is the order in which events happen. In *The Communication Story*, the author writes about how communication has changed over time. Encourage children to pay attention to the order in which communication has changed, from the oldest forms to how we communicate today.

TEXT STRUCTURE Remind children that the way an author organizes a book is called *text structure*. Point out the label on page 4. Ask: What does this label tell you about this page? *(it will probably tell me how smoke was used to communicate)* Repeat with page 5. Ask: How do these labels help you as you read? *(it quickly tells me what I'll be reading about)*

ADDITIONAL SKILL INSTRUCTION

COMPARE AND CONTRAST Remind children: Alike means telling how things are the same. Different means telling how things are not the same. After children have read page 8, ask: How is using a pigeon to communicate like using the mail? How is it different? As they read the book, have children keep a list of the kinds of communication that don't need electricity and a list of the kinds that do.

Name _____

Sequence

Use the boxes below to make a picture story of three examples of how communication has changed. Make sure your pictures are in order from oldest to newest.

1.

2.

3.

Name _____

Vocabulary

Circle the picture that each word describes.

1. built

2. early

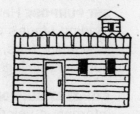   

3. learn

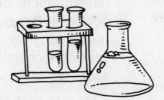   

4. science

5. through

Marla's Good Idea

SUMMARY Marla's older brothers do not want her help with their project for a science fair. Marla is hurt, but not for long. She cooks up a bubble mixture you can eat and uses a piece of wire to make a bubble wand. When her brothers find out about Marla's invention, they get an idea for an invention of their own and invite Marla to help them create it.

LESSON VOCABULARY

answered	carry
different	poor

INTRODUCE THE BOOK

INTRODUCE THE TITLE AND AUTHOR Discuss with children the title and the author of *Marla's Good Idea*. Based on the title, ask students to say what they think the book will be about. Have them notice the picture on the cover and ask what they think Marla's idea will involve.

BUILD BACKGROUND Ask children if they have ever invented anything. Ask them to describe their inventions. Ask them if they have any ideas for inventions. Ask them to think about the materials they would need and where they would get them.

PREVIEW/TAKE A PICTURE WALK Invite children to look through the pictures in the selection. Ask them to point out details they think are interesting. Ask: What questions do you have as you look at the pictures in this book?

READ THE BOOK

SET PURPOSE Have students set a purpose for reading *Marla's Good Idea*. Children's interest in science fairs, inventions, and relationships between siblings should guide this purpose.

STRATEGY SUPPORT: INFERRING Tell children that inferring is using information in the story to make a guess about something the author didn't tell you. Readers can often infer things from the photographs or illustrations in the story. Encourage children to make inferences as they read the story. After page 3, ask: What do you think Marla's big brother is like? How can you tell?

COMPREHENSION QUESTIONS

PAGE 3 What are Marla's brothers doing? *(making something for the science fair)*

PAGE 4 Why do Marla's brothers think she can't help them? *(They think she is too young and does not have good ideas.)*

PAGE 4 What does the picture on this page tell you about the brothers' work so far? What details in the picture tell you this? *(Possible response: They have been trying many ideas; science tools and equipment lie around, telescope on table, a plan is taped to the wall.)*

PAGE 5 How did Marla feel when her brothers told her to go away? *(so unhappy she almost started to cry)*

PAGE 11 How are Marla's idea and Mike's idea alike and different? *(Alike: Both ideas involve blowing bubbles that can be eaten. Different: Marla used a wand to blow bubbles of one flavor; Mike wants to build a machine that will blow bubbles of many flavors.)*

PAGE 11 What did Marla's brothers come to understand about where good ideas come from? *(Possible response: Good ideas can come from the most familiar people and things around you.)*

REVISIT THE BOOK

THINK AND SHARE

1. Possible response: Anybody can have a good idea. Even though Marla is just a kid, she comes up with a good idea.
2. Responses will vary.
3. Children should follow the directions to create the cards and use them to tell a story to a partner using the vocabulary words.
4. Children should tell about an idea for an invention they have had.

EXTEND UNDERSTANDING Invite children to look at the picture on page 3 and the one on page 11. Invite them to compare and contrast the pictures. What do they show about the difference between Marla and her brothers at the beginning of the book and Marla and her brothers at the end of the book?

RESPONSE OPTIONS

WRITING Invite children to write about a time they had a problem with a brother, sister, or good friend. What was the problem? Did the problem get solved? Who solved the problem and how?

SOCIAL STUDIES CONNECTION

Time For SOCIAL STUDIES

Students can learn more about school science fairs by visiting the library or using the Internet. Invite them to find out about winning student inventions. Invite them to tell the class about the information they found in their research.

Skill Work

TEACH/REVIEW VOCABULARY

Have students find the word *poor* in the selection. Invite them to explain the meaning of the word as it is used in this sentence. Ask them if they can think of another word with a similar meaning that could substitute for *poor* in this sentence. Continue in a similar fashion with the other vocabulary words.

TARGET SKILL AND STRATEGY

THEME Remind children that the "big idea" or lesson a story teaches is called the *theme*. Ask: When you read this story, what did it tell you about people? Does this story remind you of anything that happened to you? What is the big idea of this story? *(Possible response: You should give other people's ideas a chance.)*

ELL Invite children to fill out word webs on feelings. Invite them to brainstorm words for feelings. Challenge them to include as many different words for feelings as they can think of. Have them read their word webs to each other.

INFERRING Remind children that when they infer, they use information in the story to make a guess about something the author didn't tell them. Have children turn to page 4. Ask: How are Mike and Dan feeling on this page? How do you know? *(Possible response: I think they are frustrated with their own ideas. I know this because there are lots of crumbled pieces of paper on the floor.)*

ADDITIONAL SKILL INSTRUCTION

SEQUENCE Remind children that sequence is what happens first, next, and last. Invite them to create a time line and use it to track the sequence of events in the book. They may wish to illustrate their time line to show different events.

Name_____

Theme

Read the story.

> Marco and Sam raced home from summer camp. Sam had spent the summer playing basketball and Marco had spent the summer taking a science class.
>
> "How was the last day?" their mom asked.
>
> "Great!" Sam said, "but we didn't win the trophy this year."
>
> "It was amazing!" Marco said, "but my science report didn't win an award."
>
> "Awards and trophies are nice," said their mom, "but you both came home with something even better."
>
> "What's that?" the boys asked.
>
> "A great experience!"

What is the big idea of this story?

_____
- -
_____
- -
_____
- -
_____
- -
_____

Name_____

Vocabulary

Read the paragraph below. Fill in each blank with the correct vocabulary word.

> **Words to Know**
>
> answered   carry
> different   poor

"Help us _____ this box into the basement," they said.

We each took a _____ corner.

In the basement, we opened the box. I found some of my old toys.

"Look at this _____ doll," I said. "She is missing one eye! What will happen to her?"

"Don't worry," Jeff _____. "Mom says she will be repaired."

T-Chart

Suggestions You can use this chart to record information in two categories or for various sorting activities. Write the heading at the top of each column.

Three-Column Chart

Suggestions You can use this chart to record information in three categories or for various sorting activities. Write the heading at the top of each column.

Classify

Suggestions Children can use this chart to classify information. For example, pictures of animals could be placed in the circle and then sorted into land animals and water animals in the boxes below.

Pictograph

Title _____

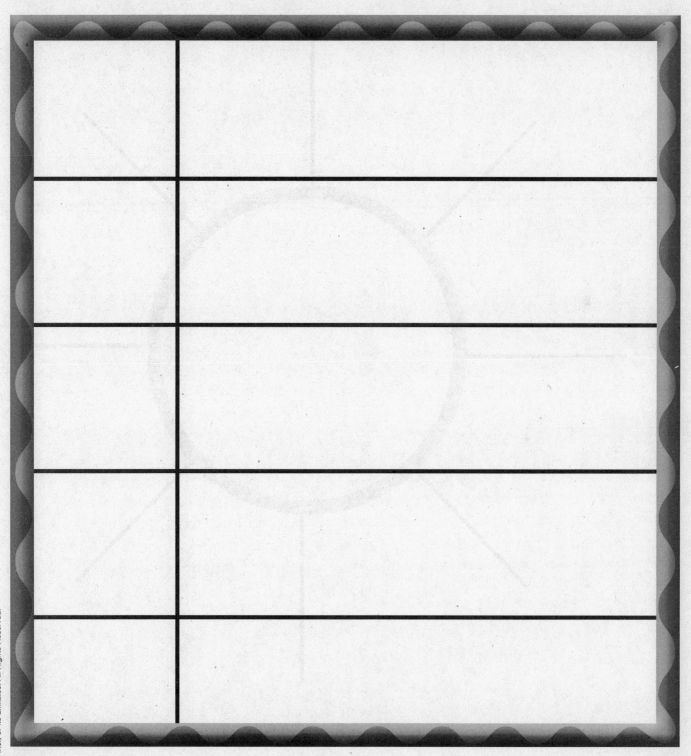

Suggestions Help children make a pictograph to record information. Children draw simple pictures on the chart or on self-stick notes to represent each item. Record the topic at the top of the chart. Some possible topics are: *What did we have for lunch? What pets do we have? What color shoes are we wearing?*

Web A

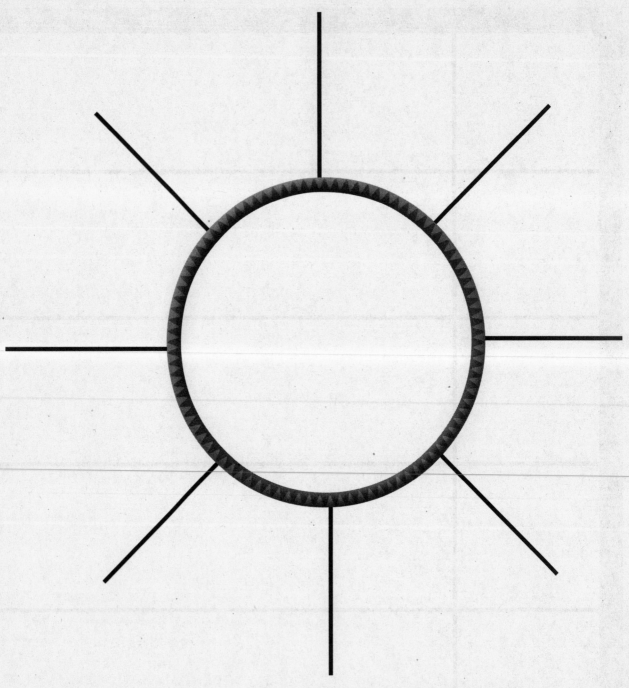

Suggestions You can use this chart to activate children's prior knowledge about a topic. Write a major concept in the circle such as *Pets* or *Machines.* Children write or dictate words or ideas that relate to the concept. Write them so that the lines connect them to the circle.

Web B

Suggestions You can use this chart to activate children's prior knowledge about a topic. Write a major concept in the middle circle, such as *Things at School*. In the smaller circles, children dictate words or ideas that relate to the concept. Additional ideas may be added on spokes coming from the smaller circles.

KWL Chart

K **What We Know**	W **What We Want to Know**	L **What We Learned**

Suggestions Have children tell what they know or think they know about the topic. Record their responses in the column **What We Know.** Ask children what they would like to learn. List their questions in **What We Want to Know.** After children learn more about the topic, discuss what they learned. List children's responses in **What We Learned.**

Prediction

_____

_____

_____

_____

_____

Suggestions You can use this chart to help children discuss predictions. Have children suggest what might happen next in a story or other situation. Children may draw a picture and dictate sentences to show the prediction.

Sequence

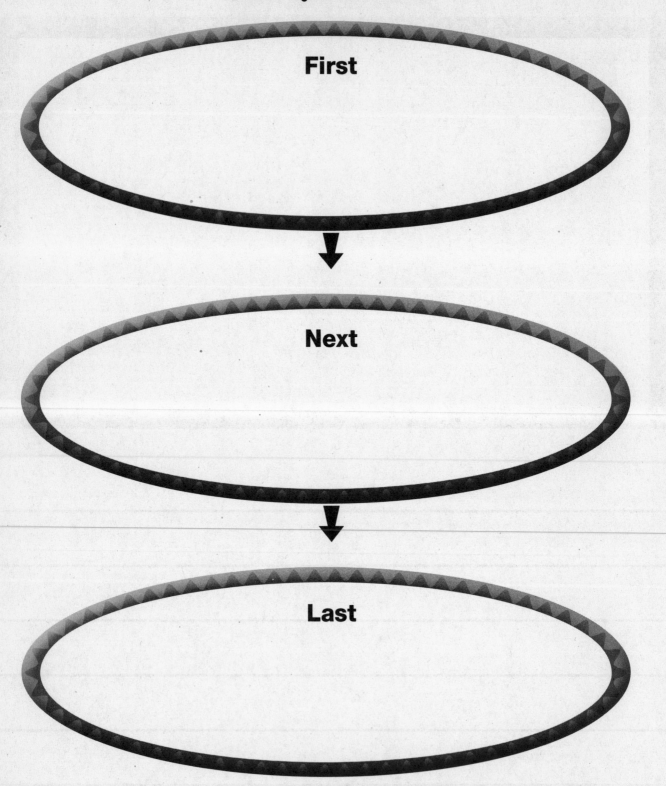

First

Next

Last

Suggestions Use this chart to help children place events in sequence. Children can draw pictures or dictate what happened first, next, and last.

Story Sequence A

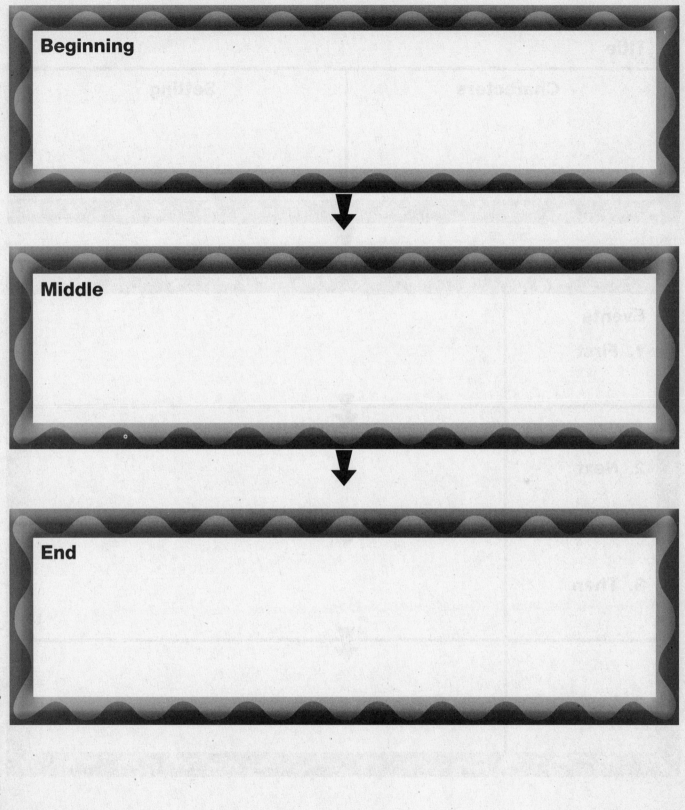

Beginning

Middle

End

Suggestions Use this chart to help children place events in a story in sequence. Children can draw pictures or dictate what happened in the beginning, middle, and end.

Story Sequence B

Title		
Characters		**Setting**

Events

1. First

2. Next

3. Then

4. Last

Suggestions After recording the title, characters, and setting of a story, children chart the sequence of events. This organizer helps children understand how one event leads to another.

Book Report

Title _____

Author _____

Illustrator _____

Setting _____

Characters _____

Our Favorite Parts _____

Suggestions You can use this chart to record information about a big book or trade book. Discuss where the story takes place, what happens in the book, and how children feel about the book. Invite children to draw pictures of their favorite parts of the book.

Story Comparison

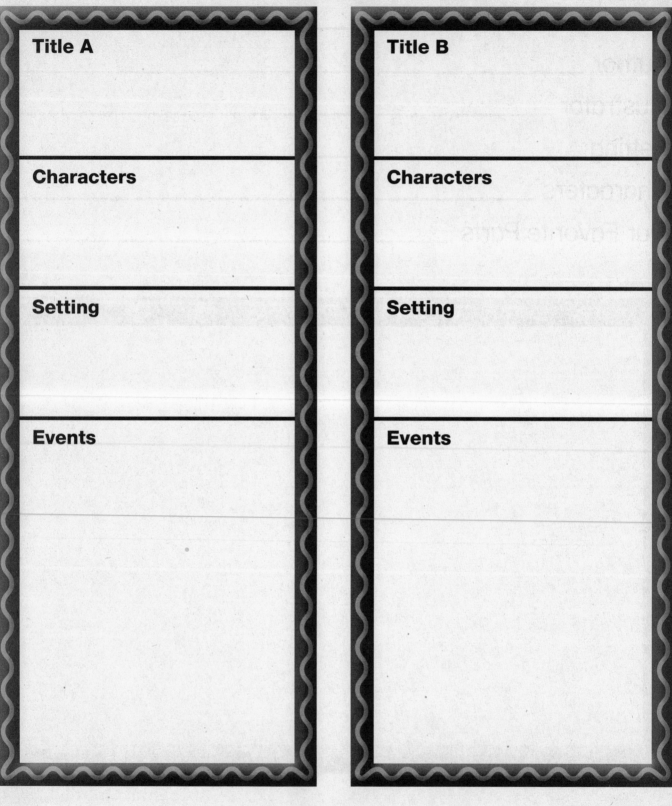

Title A

Characters

Setting

Events

Title B

Characters

Setting

Events

Suggestions Use this chart to help children compare story elements and structures. This type of activity prepares children for working with Venn diagrams. Children may illustrate or dictate these comparisons.

Question the Author

Title _____

Author _____ Page _____

1. What does the author tell you?	
2. Why do you think the author tells you that?	
3. Does the author say it clearly?	
4. What would make it clearer?	
5. How would you say it instead?	

Suggestions Use this chart to help children understand the author's purpose and the author's craft. Students analyze what was said, how well it was said, and how it might be said differently.

Main Idea

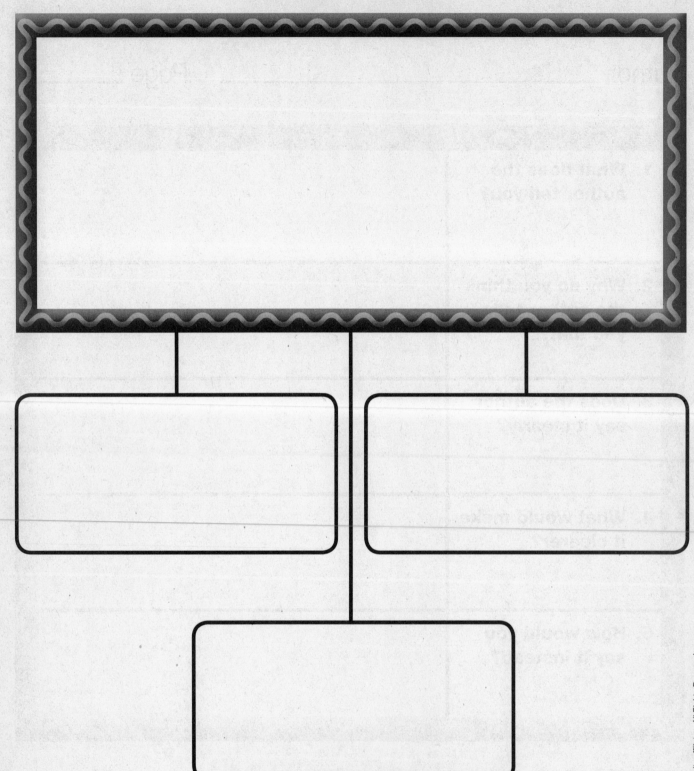

 Suggestions Use this chart to help children understand the main idea of what they read. Ask: *What is the story all about?* Write children's responses in the top box. Have children draw or dictate in the smaller boxes other things they remember from the story.

Venn Diagram

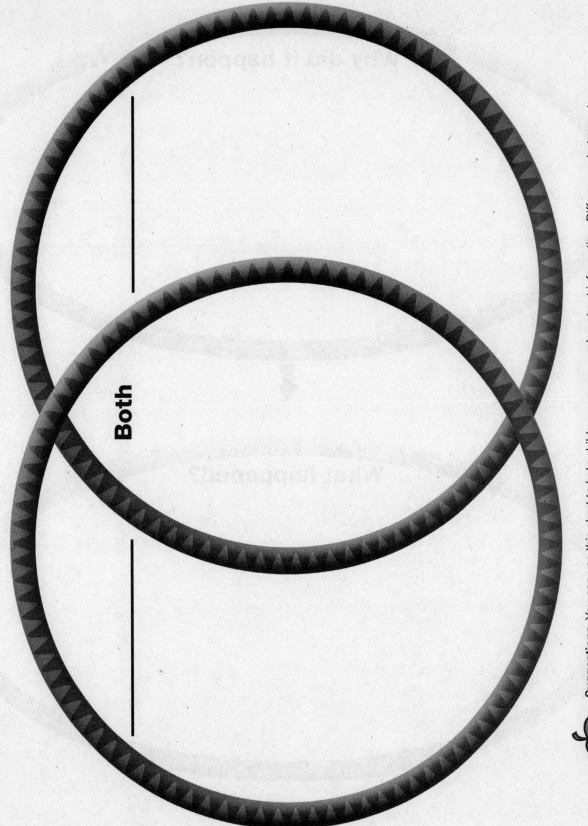

Both

Suggestions You can use this chart to help children compare and contrast information. Differences between two things being compared should be written in the non-intersecting portions. Similarities between two things being compared should be written in the intersection.

Venn Diagram **147**

Cause and Effect

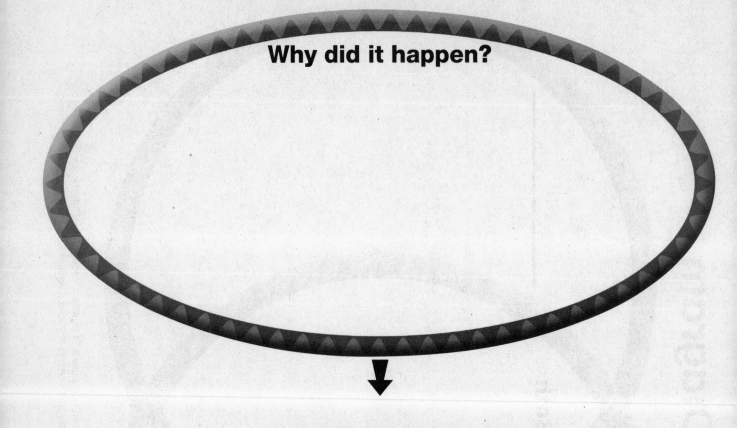

Why did it happen?

What happened?

Suggestions Use this chart to help children understand what happens (effect) and why it happens (cause). Children draw pictures in the appropriate ovals or dictate sentences to show an event. Help children think back and describe or draw what caused that event to happen.

Cycle Chart

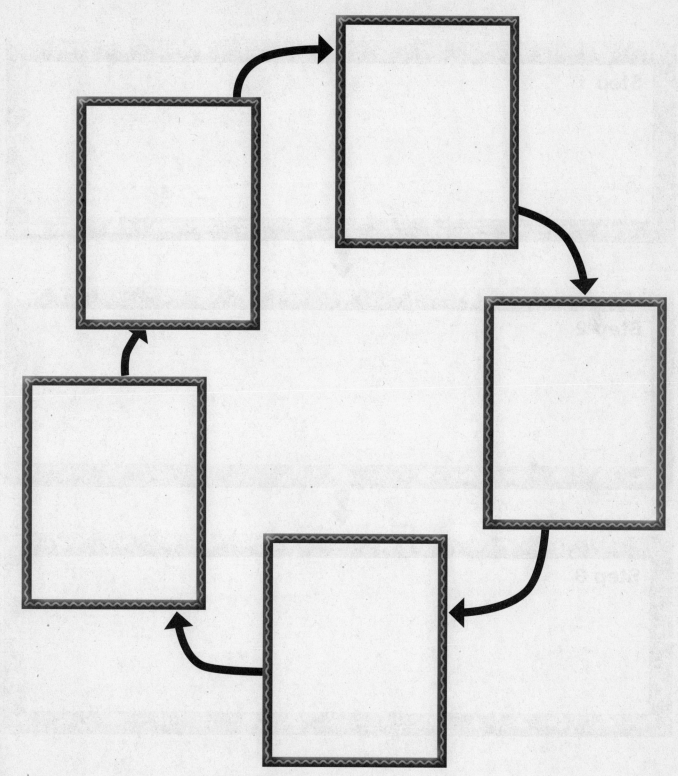

Suggestions Use this chart to help children understand how a series of events produces a series of results again and again. Discuss such questions as: *How does one event lead to another? What is the final outcome?* This chart works well for depicting life cycles.

Steps in a Process

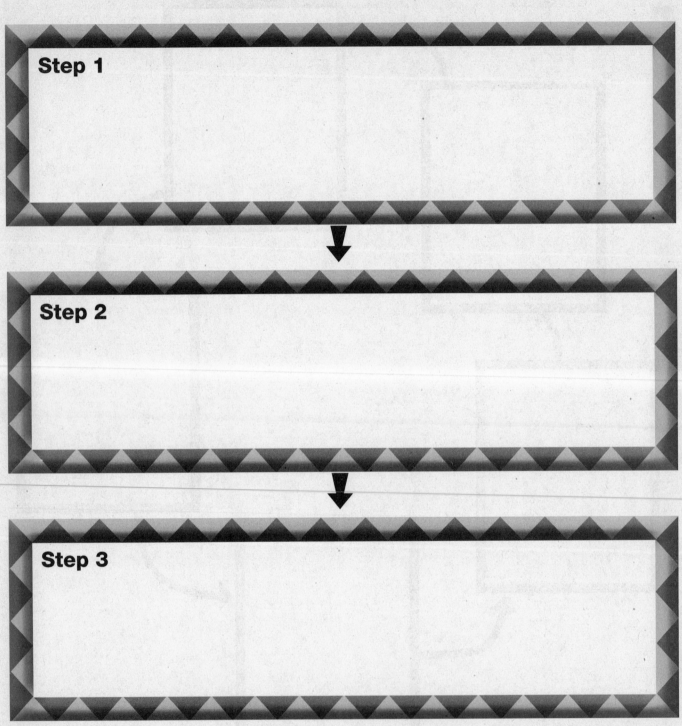

Step 1

Step 2

Step 3

Suggestions Use this chart to help children break down a process. This chart works well with a how-to activity that has a few simple steps. Students may draw pictures or dictate how to do something.

Writing Topics

Family	Friends	Pets

Hobbies	Favorite Activities

Special Places	Favorite Vacations

Happy Times	Times I Felt Proud

 Suggestions Use this chart as a writing resource or interest inventory. Over time, children can generate numerous topics for future compositions.

Letter Format

_____

Dear _____,

_____
- -
_____
- -
_____
- -
_____
- -
_____
- -
_____
- -
_____
- -

_____
- - - - - - - - - - - - - - - - - - ,
_____
- - - - - - - - - - - - - - - - - -

Suggestions Use this organizer to help children understand the format of a letter. The format can be used for writing to friends, family, or characters from a story.

Numbered List

Title _____

1. _____

2. _____

3. _____

4. _____

5. _____

Suggestions Use this chart to help children list characters, settings, problems, or items that can be found in different contexts or categories.

Answer Key

Leveled Reader Practice Pages

Mack and Zack p. 14

🎯 **CHARACTER AND SETTING**

1. Drawings will vary, but top drawing should reveal Zack's affection for Mack, and bottom drawing should show a house.
2. Possible response: a nice cat

Mack and Zack p. 15 Vocabulary

1. come
2. way
3. in
4. on
5. my

The Sick Pets p. 18

🎯 **PLOT**

Beginning box should show a rabbit in a garden; Middle box should show a rabbit with a carrot; End box should show a rabbit and a dog.

The Sick Pets p. 19 Vocabulary

Make sure children find all the vocabulary words within the word search.

Where They Live p. 22

🎯 **CHARACTER AND SETTING**

1. Drawings will vary but should depict events from the country.
2. Drawings will vary but should depict events from the city.

Where They Live p. 23 Vocabulary

1. from
2. get
3. Help
4. glue
5. use
6. little

Which Fox? p. 26

1. a fox in the woods
2. a fox in the zoo
3. look
4. gets

Which Fox? p. 27 Vocabulary

1. eat
2. four
3. this
4. too
5. eat, her, this, five

What Animals Can You See? p. 30

🎯 **MAIN IDEAS AND DETAILS**

1. b
2. c
3. a

What Animals Can You See? p. 31 Vocabulary

1. tree
2. small
3. saw
4. your
5. Drawings will vary but should show a bird leaving a nest.

Which Animals Will We See? p. 34

🎯 **CAUSE AND EFFECT**

1. b
2. a
3. c
4. Possible response: I went to school because it was Monday.

Which Animals Will We See? p. 35 Vocabulary

1. into
2. them
3. home
4. many
5. home

Let's Go to the Zoo p. 38

🎯 **SEQUENCE**

1–3. Drawings will vary but should in the order of the story.

Let's Go to the Zoo p. 39 Vocabulary
1. want
2. no
3. good
4. catch
5. put
6. said

A Class p. 42
🔘 **CAUSE AND EFFECT**
It was time to go home.
The kids go on the school bus.
Drawings will vary but should show children on a school bus.

A Class p. 43 Vocabulary
1. paper
2. be
3. old
4. horse
5. could

Look at My Neighborhood p. 46
🔘 **AUTHOR'S PURPOSE**
Possible response: The author wanted people to know that cities have parks.

Look at My Neighborhood p. 47 Vocabulary
1. people
2. out
3. work
4. live
5. Who

The Dinosaur Herds p. 50
🔘 **SEQUENCE**
1–3.   Drawings will vary but should reflect correct sequence of events

The Dinosaur Herds p. 51 Vocabulary
1. inside
2. together
3. there
4. down
5. now

People Help the Forest p. 54
🔘 **AUTHOR'S PURPOSE**
1. forest
2. help
3. look
4. safe

People Help the Forest p. 55 Vocabulary
1. water
2. grow
3. food
4. find
5. under
Mystery word: around

Honey p. 58
🔘 **COMPARE AND CONTRAST**
1. honey
2. One paragraph is about people eating honey when they are sick. The other paragraph is about people using honey in the bath.

Honey p. 59 Vocabulary
1. Some
2. Other
3. also
4. family
5. Their
6. new
7. Possible response: My family bought a new car.

Let's Build a Park! p. 62
🔘 **SEQUENCE**
a. 3
b. 5
c. 4
d. 1
e. 2
Responses will vary but should reflect understanding of text and illustrations in the story.

Let's Build a Park! p. 63 Vocabulary
1. things
2. always
3. stays
4. everything
5. day
6. become
7. Nothing

Mac Can Do It! p. 66
🔘 **COMPARE AND CONTRAST**
Possible response:
Mac: baby, smart
Both: happy
Mom and Dad: adults

Mac Can Do It! p. 67 Vocabulary
Make sure children find all the vocabulary words within the word search.

Big Wishes and Her Baby p. 70
FACT AND OPINION
1. b and d
2–3. Possible response: The food helps the baby horse grow. It is important to make young horses comfortable around people.

Big Wishes and Her Baby p. 71 Vocabulary
very
our
car
house
school, away
friends

Plans Change p. 74
AUTHOR'S PURPOSE
1. helmet
2. safety
3. cars
4. bike

Plans Change p. 75 Vocabulary
1. Read
2. few
3. Soon
4. how
5. again
6. afraid

Let's Visit a Butterfly Greenhouse p. 78
FACT AND OPINION
Possible responses:
1. Caterpillars are interesting.
2. I like to watch butterflies fly.

Let's Visit a Butterfly Greenhouse p. 79
Vocabulary
1. 8
2. 5
3. 6
4. 4
5. 10
6. Possible response: I know I would enjoy going to a butterfly garden.

Seasons Come and Go p. 82
DRAW CONCLUSIONS
Possible responses:
1. The fox will be hard to see because it blends in with the snow.
2. The fox will be protected because it blends in with the ground.

Seasons Come and Go p. 83 Vocabulary
1. Before
2. does
3. won't
4. right
5. good-bye
6. Oh

Special Days, Special Food p. 86
DRAW CONCLUSIONS
1. love to make and eat special foods.
2. you have to eat them to find out what's inside.
3. you find it in your piece of cake.
4. they make colorful shakes out of it.
5. there are many foods, dancing, and music.

Special Days, Special Food p. 87 Vocabulary
1. about
2. surprised
3. gives
4. worry
5. enjoy
6. surprise
7. Would

The Art Show p. 90
THEME
Beginning: Matt draws a picture of Sam.
Middle: Sam scribbles on Matt's drawing.
End: Matt's picture wins a ribbon at the art show.
What Matt learns: Possible response: A picture does not need to be perfect to be good.

The Art Show p. 91 Vocabulary
1. draw
2. colors
3. drew
4. great
5. show
6. sign
7. over

Treasures of Our Country p. 94

1. a, b, d
2. Possible response: It is 630 feet tall. It took two years to build.

Treasures of Our Country p. 95

1. Once
2. Wild
3. took
4. found
5. mouth

A Visit to the Ranch p. 98

MAIN IDEA

1. She never petted a horse before.
2. They laughed when they got wet.
3. The moon rose in the sky when they were riding.
4. The girls tied good knots.
5. Lia said city life sounded like fun.

A Visit to the Ranch p. 99 Vocabulary

1. laugh
2. moon
3. eight
4. touch
5. above

Drawings and sentences will differ but should be humorous.

My Little Brother Drew p. 102

THEME

1. Sue learns how to help Drew do things.
2. Showing how to do something is the best way to teach.
3. Drawings will differ but should show Sue helping Drew.

My Little Brother Drew p. 103 Vocabulary

Sentences will vary but should show an understanding of the vocabulary word.

1. stood
2. picture
3. room
4. thought
5. remember

The Story of the Kids Care Club p. 106

CAUSE AND EFFECT

1. The neighbor could not rake the leaves herself.
2. Some people did not have enough to eat.
3. Kids wanted to help others
4. The older people are lonely.
5. so that they could give them to children in need

The Story of the Kids Care Club p. 107

Vocabulary

1. c
2. e
3. b
4. a
5. d
6. f
7. g

Squirrel and Bear p. 110

CHARACTER, SETTING, AND PLOT

Drawings and sentences will vary but should show Bear helping Squirrel move with an explanation of the drawing.

Squirrel and Bear p. 111 Vocabulary

1. behind
2. never
3. eyes
4. pulling
5. behind, along, toward

Puppy Raiser p. 114

DRAW CONCLUSIONS

1. caring, friendly
2. cross the street; travel
3. to work; to school; to a restaurant
4. Possible response: smart, friendly

Puppy Raiser p. 115 Vocabulary

1. should
2. loved
3. wood
4. door

A Mighty Oak Tree p. 118

COMPARE AND CONTRAST

1. They both eat acorns.
2. They both live in oak trees.
3. Birds don't eat acorns, squirrels do.
4. Bears don't live in trees, squirrels do.

A Mighty Oak Tree p. 119 Vocabulary

1. among
2. instead
3. none
4. Another
5. among, another, instead, none

Simple Machines at Work p. 122

MAIN IDEA

Inclined Plane
Simple Machines

Simple Machines at Work p. 123 Vocabulary

1. kinds
2. against, heavy
3. heavy, against
4. today
5. goes
6. b
7. b
8. a
9. a
10. c

The Communication Story p. 126

SEQUENCE

Drawings will differ but should be in sequential order.

The Communication Story p. 127 Vocabulary

1. house
2. 6:00 am
3. the girl reading
4. the beaker and test tubes
5. the boy walking through in the door

Marla's Good Idea p. 130

THEME

Possible response: It's nice to get awards and trophies, but it's more important to have a good experience.

Marla's Good Idea p. 131 Vocabulary

carry
different
poor
answered